From the depth of the Heart in America

Abul Hasan Ali Nadwi

Nadwi Press

2022 CE – 1443 H

Translation of the Qur'ān

It should be perfectly clear that the Qur'ān is only authentic in its original language, Arabic. Since perfect translation of the Qur'ān is impossible, we have used the translation of the meaning of the Qur'ān throughout the book, as the result is only a crude meaning of the Arabic text.

Qur'ānic verses appear in speech marks proceeded by a reference to the Surah and verse number. Sayings (*Hadith*) of Prophet Muhammad (saw) appear in inverted commas along with reference to the Hadith Book and its Reporter.

CONTENTS

FOREWORD

In the Name of Allah, the Beneficent, the Merciful

This is a collection of my speeches in the United States and Canada which I visited in the summer of 1977. I went there at the invitation of Muslim Students Association, mainly to attend its Annual Conference at Bloomington in Indiana. After the Conference, a tour was arranged by the Association which took me to almost all the important cities and educational, cultural and industrial centres of North America where a considerable number of Muslims drawn from India, Pakistan and the Arab countries live for various reasons. The original itinerary included New York City, Jersey City, Philadelphia, Baltimore, Boston, Chicago, Detroit, Salt Lake City, San Francisco, San Jose and Los Angeles in the States, and Montreal and Toronto in Canada, to which Washington was added later.

In all, I addressed twenty gatherings, half of them in Arabic and half in Urdu. I had an opportunity of speak at five leading American Universities—the Columbia University at New York, the Harvard University at Cambridge, the Detroit University at Ann Arbor, the South Californian University at Los Angeles and the Utah University at Salt Lake City—,and was, also, asked to give the Friday sermon in the Prayer Hall at United Nations Headquarters and in the Jami' Masjids of Toronto and Detroit. Muslims who are studying in America or have taken up residence there took a keen interest in the meetings and came from far and near to attend them.

In the haste and hurry of moving from place to place it was not possible to collect the tapes of all the speeches. The transcriptions contained in this volume were prepared, largely, by Syed Mushtaq Ahmad Bhopali of Darul Uloon Nadwatul

Uluma, Lucknow, from the tapes I was able to bring with me. Before I could revise the written copies of the speeches, most of them were published in *Tamir-i-Hayat*, the fortnightly organ of Nadwatul Uluma, for which I am thankful to its Editor, Ishaq Jalis Nadwi. Had the printed versions of the speeches not been made available to me, it would have taken much more time and labour to prepare the persent volume. The speeches in Arabic, except for the translations of two of them, have **not** been included in this collection.   These will be published separately from Beirut or Cairo.

It is hoped that this booklet will be read with interest both in India and abroad, and friends residing in America who had listened to the speeches directly as well as those who could not or did not do so will find something in them deserving of serious thought.

For fellow countrymen it is a 'gift' of the trip to America and for the friends and well-wishers in America, a 'requital' of the kindness and affection shown by them.

If there is any justification for the publication of these speeches it is the attempt at plain-speaking that has been made in them. My constant endeavour had been to speak straight from the heart, without mincing the matters, and to offer some sincere suggestion to the Muslim brothers and sisters who have settled in the West, particularly in America. As for the Western Civilisation, it has been viewed from a height which Islam confers upon its followers and from which both the Old and the New Worlds seem narrow and empty, and their glitter false and unreal. The credit for this particular way of looking at things does not belong to me but to the Guidance and Message which imparts a new vision to man and causes the scales to fall from his eyes.

I take the opportunity to express my sincere gratitude to all the friends who helped to make the journey such a rewarding experience and looked after my needs and comforts with unceasing care and affection. They make a long list, but mention must be made of the names of Syed Naziruddin Ali Hyderabadi, the Vice-President and Programme-Incharge, Mr. Anis Ahmad, the Director of Education, Publicity and Information, Dr. Mahmud Rushdan, the General Secretary, and Dr. Yaqub Mirza, the President of the Muslim Students Association who spared no pains to make my stay as useful and comfortable as possible.

My Allah requite them bounteously and bestow His good pleasure upon them.

ABUL HASAN ALI NADWI

Daira-i-Shah Alamullah
Rae Bareli
December 20, 1977

PART ONE
WESTERN CIVILISATION AN AMERICAN WAY OF LIFE

★ STUDY ★ APPRAISAL ★ ANALYSIS

DISCOVERY OF AMERICA

The speech was delivered at the Muslim Community Centre, Chicago on June 19, 1977, before a large gathering of educated Muslims.

I

Allama Iqbal opens his long Persian poem, *Asrar-i-Khudi* (Secrets of the Self), with these verses from Maulana Jalaluddin Rumi.

> Last night the Sheikh wandered about the town with a lamp
>
> Saying, "I am tired of demon and beast; man is my desire.
>
> My heart is sick of the feeble-spirited fellow-travellers;
>
> The Loin of God[1] and Rustam-i-Dastaan[2] are my desire."
>
> I said, "We, too, searched for him, but he couldn't be found."
>
> He replied, "What cannot be found that thing is my desire."

On a dark night, Maulana Rumi tells, a sage was wandering in the streets of the town, with a lamp in hand, as if he was searching for something that had been lost. The poet enquired from him what he was trying to find, and he replied that he had grown sick of living in what, in truth, was the abode of wild animals, and was now looking for man, a Lion of God and a Rustam-i-Dastaan, who could restore his faith in humanity. The poet remarked, "You are looking for the impossible; for something

---

1. Meaning Hazrat Ali.
2. Rustam son of Zal (nicknamed Dastaan) was a famous hero of pre-Islamic Persia.

that does not exist. Rest assured, you are never going to find him." "It is the rare, the uncommon, the unattainable that I seek. This is the trouble with me," replied the wise, old man.

As you know, I have come here at the invitation of the Muslim Students Association and it is a new world for me, not, of course, in the sense in which it was for Columbus, but from the viewpoint of a student who, also, possesses some knowledge of religion. I am grateful to the Muslim Students Association for giving me an opportunity not only of coming to this great land. but, also, of seeing it from coast to coast and of meeting people and speaking to them. I have travelled from New York to California, and, also, visited Canada, thus covering about four thousand miles during these few weeks. It is at the end of the tour that I am addressing this meeting. You will, naturally, like to know my impressions. Coming, as I do, from a country which, so to speak, is backward at present and lagging behind the West, I would have described to you with relish the phenomenal advancement that has taken place here, but you are more familiar with it than me, and, hence, it will be unnecessary.

To many of you the verses from Maulana Rum I have just quoted will have come as a surprise. Maulana Rum lived in Anatolia which was not backward. On the other hand, it was one of the most advanced parts of the then civilised world. The Maulana belonged to a place where the foundations of the magnificent Saljuk Kingdom were about to be laid. He was born at Balkh, in Iran, which was the most civilised country in those days and could, justly, be called the Greece of the East, In philosophy and literature it had made a glorious contribution and left an imperishable mark on the pages of history. Nevertheless, he has tried to show the wounds of his heart through these verses. He relates the story of the "sage", but in fact, it is his own story. He says that in that wonderful city and in that land of culture and enlightenment, he pines for man. There is everything there—stately mansions, blooming gardens, delicious food, elegant dresses and refined manners, but not man. What one sees are not real men; they possess only human forms and figures.

In another verse, Maulana Rum has spoken with greater clarity. He says :

These are not men, only men's faces they have,
Slaves of the stomach, victims of sensuality.

The bloom of the machines

I have seen of America what could be seen during this brief stay and have travelled from north to south and from east to west, but the one thing that has struck me is the supremacy of the machines. The bloom you see here is the bloom of mathematics, trade and technology. The physical sciences have reached the highest point of their development and given to mankind whatever they could by way of progress, ease and luxury.

But what will the answer be if in this country which is bustling with life and activity one were to ask how many real men lived; men whose hearts throbbed and eyes wept for the sake of humanity; men who controlled their carnal desires and were the riders and not the mounts of this civilisation; who held the reins of life instead of being driven by it; who knew their Creator and whose hearts were filled with love for Him and respect for mankind; who led a simple life, in harmony with nature, and were aware of true joys and genuine pleasures; who did not like tensions and conflicts in the world and hated the selfishness and greed of the politicians; who wished every country well and wanted it to prosper; who were eager to give and not to grab; who did not believe that the aim of life was only to eat, drink and be merry, but thought that there was much more pleasure in feeding the other man and going hungry themselves than in eating the most sumptuous meal; who saw gain in loss and victory in defeat; who dreamt of the reconstruc-tion of the world and were not concerned solely with the growth and development of their own land; who wanted to see the world united, not on the transitory and artificial platform of the United Nations, but on the real and natural stage of the oneness of mankind; who knew what was the beginning and the end of their existence, and were, also, regardful of it; who realised that they had been created by someone and would not turn to dust, like the insects, after completing the span of their life, but had to go somewhere and render an account of the tremendous capabilities God had endowed them with, capabilities which had enabled them to impart life to stones, conquer the vastness of the skies, imprison the rays of the sun and plant their feet on the moon, and felt that the glory of man did not lie in breathing life into inanimate matter and subjugating the world through it, but in enlivening himself? God had created man and placed the crown of Vicegerency on his head : it was, therefore, not the height of his achievement that he became a slave to matter but made the matter his slave, or, rather, the slave of God and took from it the task of the fulfilment of His Will. This was what Vicegerency of God meant. Men who did not see greatness in subjugating the other countries and making them bow to their will but wanted to serve mankind selflessly and put an end to exploitation of one country or community by the other; men who aspired to release humanity from the bondage of the inordinate appetites of power, wealth and even intellect ?

The bedouin of Arabia whose head Islam had raised as high as the heavens had told Rustam, the Commander-in-Chief of Iran, bluntly that "we have been sent by Allah to deliver whom He wills from the overlordship of His slaves (i. e., men) to His own overlordship, from the narrow confines of the world to its boundlessness, and from the oppressiveness of other religions to the fairness and justice of Islam." Now, there was the mighty Rustam whose name was enough to strike terror in the heart of the enemy, and, before him, it had become possible for a poor bedouin to stand up and say : "God has appointed us to rescue men from the worship of fellow-men and lead them to the worship of no one save Him; to take them out of the prison-cell to which you have given the imposing name of the Iranian Empire into the Lord's wide and limitless world and into the open air of freedom. We take pity not on ourselves, but on you. It is your wretchedness that has evoked sympathy in our hearts and compelled us to come out of the desert-land of Arabia. Unfortunate Iranians, we want to bring you out of the golden cage in which you are held in captivity like the nightingales into the boundless kingdom of the Lord. You are the slaves of your desires and habits, of your musicians, cooks and water-men, while we are the slaves of God. We have come to deliver you from the countless forms and varieties of servility to freedom''.

Light is one, darkness has numerous faces

Freedom is one; servility is of many kinds, Light is one, but darkness has numerous faces. Hence. wherever *Noor* (Light) is mentioned in the Quran, it is in the singular number. As for instance, *Allah is the Protecting Friend of those who believe. He bringeth them out of Zulumaat*[1] *into Noor.* (II : 257)

But why ? Is the plural form of *Noor* not found in the Arabic language ? Or, was the range of expression of the Quran limited ? The fact is that light is one, while 'darknesses' are unlimited. The origin of *Noor* is one and it is the awareness of God There is no other source of guidance if Light is not available from that eternal fountainhead. Today, as I see this country, the following verses from Iqbal come to my mind, Iqbal had not visited the United States, but his knowledge of the West was deeper than ours. He says :

Though Europe is radiant with the light of knowledge,
The 'Ocean of Darkness' is barren of the 'Fount of Life'.
A nation unblessed by Divine Light,
Steam and electricity bound its works.

---

1. Plural of *Zulmat,* meaning darkness.

The West is an 'Ocean of Darkness in which the 'Fount of Life' does not exist.   There is an old proverb that the 'Fountain of Life' is found in the 'Ocean of Darkness'. It is said that Alexander had made Khwaja Khizr[1] his guide and requested him to take him to the waters of immortality in the 'Ocean of Darkness', but even Khizr had confessed his inability. Alluding to this brief story, Iqbal observes that though the West is an ·Ocean of Darkness', it does not possess the 'Fountain of Life'. What, then, is the ultimate fate of the nation which is deprived of Divine beneficence and turns its back upon Apostleship and relies wholly upon the intellect and spends all its energies on matter, on minerals, steel and weapons, and makes the terrestrial, and not the celestial, world the sole sphere of its activities ? The matter is conquered, but not its own soul; the world is subjugated, but not the spirit of the world. The West made the material world the only field of its struggle and endeavour, and material progress the high aim and ambition of its life. In it, the West hass been eminently successful for it is the practice of the Lord that He makes His Help available, in fullest measure, to man in whatever sphere he singles out for his attention.   In whatever field a man wants to make progress, God grants him a full opportunity to go ahead.   The crux of the matter lies in choice and preference.

Christianity is unsuited to the West

Those of you who have studied the history of the West and the Western Civilisation and read J. W. Draper's *History of the Conflict between Religion and Science* will agree that when Europe was converted to Christianity and the Christian missionaries got busy in it events took such a turn that it plunged head-long into materialism. Religion could not capture its imagination for Christianity offered no encouragement to intellect, nor gave a practical guidance for the organisation of society. It wanted

---

1.   Name of a Prophet who is said to have discovered the 'Fountain of Life' and drunk of it.

to take it backwards while the European races which were eager and restless by temperament wanted to press onward. A vista of opportunity and achievement was opening before them and the competition for advancement urged them to stop at nothing. The revolution that was unfolding itself forced the European people to select for themselves a field in which they had no rivals. They could not rest content with a narrow sphere of growth and progress in which they had to abide by the Bible at each step or ask the ecclesiastics whether such and such a thing was lawful or not. It was a tragedy not only for Europe but for the whole world that Christianity fell to its lot.

If it was asked which religion was most inimical to the spirit of Europe and the natural disposition of its people, the answer would invariably be, Christianity. On the other hand, as a little thought will show, no religion could be more in keeping with its genius and capable of giving it a proper sense of direction than Islam.

According to Christianity, man is born a sinner. He is carrying the heavy load of the original sin on his head. How, then, can a Christian have faith in himself? How can a man who is feeling ashamed of himself on account of being a sinner by birth look boldly at the universe, lay bare the forces of nature, pierce the bosom of the oceans and dream of reaching the planets ?

How can a man who believes that he is a born sinner, that sin is ingrained in his nature and that he is in need of an external atonement which has to be offered on his behalf undertake with pride and courage the voyage of the discovery and conquest of nature ? Here was a contradiction the parallel of which could scarcely be found in the world. It was as if two horses had been tied to a cart, one in front of it and the other behind. The same thing happened to Europe. Two horses were fastened to it. Under the influence of climatic and other environmental factors, its spirit was eager to go forward, to do something, but the horse of Christianity was pulling it back. It was trying to take it towards monasticism. The ecclesiastics were openly preaching that earthly life was a bad business and the spiritual advancement of man lay in escape from life. If he wanted to attain salvation, he should live in mountains, dedicate his life to the Church, and practise celebacy. A perusal of Lecky's *History of European Morals* would show how people ran away from the shadow of a woman. The height of callousness was that a mother travelled a thousand miles to see her son and when the son heard that she was coming he took to heels like a man possessed and the mother had to return broken-hearted. This was the Christianity that had reached the West. In the upshot, the West decided that if it had to progress, it should not only free itself from the shackles of the Church, but also take leave of religion. Significantly enough, while the decline of the Muslim World started when it abandoned Islam, the rise of the West began when it forsook Christianity.

Slave of machines

It is this distressing evolutionary process that has, today, made America a slave of the machines. The supremacy of the United States is accepted all over the world and its hand is seen in everything that happens anywhere. No country, Muslim or non-Muslim, is altogether free from its control and domination. In one form or another, its presence is felt at every place. Plans are made here and enforced in our countries and our own leaders implement them. Today, America has enslaved the world, but it has, itself, become the slave of the machines. It is a prisoner of its way of life, of material progress, of factories and laboratories, and of fancy goods and gadgets. The thing that I did not see here was man, the real man whose heart was alive and awake, and not the working part of a machine. Man, here, has got cast so completely in the technological mould of life that his ideas and emotions, too, have become mechanical. The properties of rock and iron have entered into his soul. He has become narrow and selfish, cold, unfeeling and impervious. There is no warmth in his heart; no moisture in his eyes. This is the reality I have sadly observed during my stay in America.

Guard against the dissolution of your personality

Before I leave for home I would like to tell you one thing : do not be overawed by this civilisation. You are the fruit of the tree of Apostleship. Live here, but keep away from the slavish imitation of the Western Civilisation. Derive as much benefit as you like from your stay, but do not be swayed by crude and vulgar materialism. Remember your message and be on your guard against the dissolution of your personality. Do not feel ashamed of your Faith, way of life and culture. Do not imagine that you are the beasts and they are men. No, you are men and they are the beasts. This land is glittering with electric lights ; even the night here is bright as day ; but it is devoid of true effulgence, of blessedness and Divine guidance. As Iqbal has said :

> Dark is the Frankish country with the smoke of its machines;
> This 'valley of Blessedness and Hope' is not worthy of Divine Splendour.

Bondmen of idols carved by themselves

These people are the slaves of their habits and of the mechanical contraptions and devices made by themselves. Hazrat Ibrahim (Abraham) had asked the idol-worshippers of his time : *What are these images unto which ye pay devotion ?* (XXI : 52). What irony is it that you kneel down tomorrow before what you make today ? The same is happening here. To-day a standard is laid down, a law is formulated and a machine is made, and, tomorrow, the whole nation becomes a slave to them. Bondmen of the idols and images carved by their own hands !

Deputyship of Ibrahim

This country is an idol-hall in which the *Azan* of Ibrahim has to be given, and this you, alone, can do. You are the real descendants of Ibrahim, not the Jews who have strayed far away from his path. Not the Christians who are the followers of the Christianity of St. Paul, not of Jesus. They have been divested of true Christianity. It was a colossal conspiracy that bore fruit. No religious conspiracy has, perhaps, been so successful. It brought about a complete metamorphosis of Christianity. Now, whether Catholics or Protestants, they are the adherents of St. Paul. They have lost the claim to be the successors of Hazrat Ibrahim. You are his successor.

In the words of Iqbal :

Architect of *Haram*, for rebuilding the world awake;
Out of heavy sleep, heavy sleep arise !
Out of slumber deep arise !

Only the architects of *Haram* can build the new world. Today, destruction is rampant. In appearance it is construction, in truth, destruction. It was the mission of the Apostle you follow to deliver mankind from every kind of servility to the servility of One God. You, therefore, are in America not merely as masses of flesh and blood, nor simply as Indians, Pakistanis, Egyptians and Syrians.

Break idols of colour and blood; lose yourselves in the *Millet*.

Neither the Irani should remain nor Turani nor Afghani.

You are not Egyptians and Syrians, but Muslims You are one community, one brotherhood. You are Ibrahimi and Mohammadi. Know yourself. You have not come here to lose your identity and get fitted into this monstrous machine like a valueless part or to fill your bellies like the animals. No. Take the Message to the peoples of this land; wake them up; tell them how they have gone out of the right way.

If it ever occurs to the Western people how wrong and perverted is their outlook on life, they go to the other extreme. They turm towards Hippie-ism, Hindu asceticism and renunciation. A large bathing festival, called Kumbh, is held every year at Allahabad, in India. If you go to it, you will find educated Americans roaming about like stray cattle, or, rather, lunatics. This civilisation has developed indigestion. They have imbibed the wine of culture so excessively that they have begun to vomit. They are seeking satisfaction by descending to the level of the beasts, by rejecting the favours and blessings of God, and by running away from the realities of life. Would to God that our Islamic countries were capable of showing the correct path to the Americans and speaking to them in a confident, self-assured manner. But alas, not one of them is in that position. The result is that when the Americans get disgusted with their own way of life, they go to the Himalayas and use narcotics to produce an unreal feeling of peace and serenity. We, the Muslims, could lend guidance to them if we possessed the capability.

Where are Muslims ?

Brothers and sisters, you are not here merely to earn and spend. This any community can do. You are here to earn according to your need, but you must, also, know your station and persent before the Americans a new design of life. You should give the *Azan* which may stir their minds and offer *Namaz* so that they may see and ponder over it. Lead a clean life in order that a revulsion is created in them for their own degenerate ways of living, practise moderation so that a realisation may dawn on them of the foulness of sensuality and excessive self-indulgence, and freeing yourselves from the ruthless domination of the machines, live in a cool, calm and collected manner in order that they may know where peace is. Rediscover the world that lies within you and develop the spirituality which might be felt by those who came into contact with you. I wish that devout bondmen of the Lord, men with an illumined heart, came to live here and told these people who are disgusted with life that *Verily in the remembrance of Allah do hearts find rest.* (XIII : 28).

Today, only the Muslims can give this message, but where are they ? Has any Muslim country or community the courage to tell the Americans that *in the remembrance of Allah do hearts find rest ?* They no longer believe in it themselves. How can they convey the message of Divine Unity to others who have themselves lost faith in the power and efficacy of *Namaz*, in the truth and veracity of the *Kalima*, in the control and authority of God over gain and loss, and in the pre-ordination of good and evil, and made the Americans the great provider of the daily bread ? How can they tell them that *there is no Giver of Sustenance save Allah ?*

First, try to produce Faith within yourselves, observe *Namaz* and spend some time everyday in meditation ; produce the warmth that has been destroyed by the smoke of the factories, refresh your soul, set right the aim of your life, read the Quran daily, study the life of the Prophet and seek light from it, and, then, convey the message of the Religion of Nature to the Americans.

Only Islam is the Religion of Nature

Islam, alone, is the religion which does not frown upon human nature, but declares it to be essentially pure and flawless.

God had given a clean slate to man, a guiltless nature and an inclination towards goodness ; we have debased it. Man is, by nature, upright. Left to his natural instincts, he will follow the correct path. First, realise these truths, produce them within yourselves, in your hearts as well as in your minds, and, then, place them before the Americans. You are the people of preaching and instruction; you are the people of Apostleship, a community with a purpose, and the bearers of the Message. It dose not become you to live like two-legged animals, filling your stomachs and procreating.

Discover man

These are some of my impressions. I have spoken to you from the heart. I have seen everything in America, but man. If I have found one here, it is among you. It is not that I am unacquainted with America or the Americans. I have met them in literature, on the T. V., and over the radio. They are not strangers to me.

Find out the man who is the Vicegerent of God and for

whom the world has been created and in whose breast beats the heart which is more precious than the entire universe. All the treasures of the world and the achievements of science are nothing before an illumined heart. Produce that humanity in yourselves. You stay here is correct. It is not only justified, but also a worship and a great source of preaching and propagation of Faith. And if it is not that then I have great mis-givings. As I have said on various occasions, if you do not take full care to safeguard your religous life and arrange for the religious education and upbringing of your children and make sure that your future generations remain true to Islam then your living in this country is a sin and you are in grave danger.

> Lo ! As for those whom the angels take (in death) while they wrong themselves, (the angels) will ask : In what were ye engaged ? They will say : We were helpless in the land. (The angles) will say : Was not Allah's earth spacious that ye could have migrated therein ? (—IV : 97).

For us it is legitimate to live only in a country where we can live with our distinctive qualities and observe our duties. If it is not possible in this environment or you feel you cannot carry out your religious obligations then it is not permissible for you to reside in this land. It is your duty to see that you lived here as Muslims, with all your characteristics You should build your own society, and, also, assure that your children will remain Muslims after you, as Hazrat Yaqoob (Jacob) had done in regard to his progeny. It is set forth in the Quran :

> Or were you present when death came to Yaqoob, when he said unto his sons : What will you worship after me ? They said : We shall worship thy God, the God of thy fathers, Ibrahim and Ismail (Ishmael)...........(II : 133).

It was then that Hazrat Yaqoob was satisfied and he departed from the world with a contented heart. It is the duty of all of us to make certain that our children grow up to be Muslims, otherwise, friends, it will be necessary to have a second look at your stay and to decide whether you should continue to live in this country or not.

You must live as Muslims

I highly appreciate the services of MSA and other institutions and individuals who strive in the cause of Faith, form study circles, circulate the Islamic literature and organise meetings. Whether they are Arabs or non-Arabs, they are a blessed lot. God will accept their services and raise them in ranks. Of foremost importance, however, is the stipulation that you made sure you would be able to live here as Muslims and not break up and lose your identity. Would you melt like wax before the heat of this civilisation ? In that case, you would better go back to your native lands, no matter whether you earned only a fourth or a fiftieth part of what you do here. And if you are safe against it and there is no such danger then blessed is your stay in America. A new light may come to it through you, and the path may be opened for Islam.

THE HISTORY OF THE WORLD WOULD HAVE BEEN DIFFERENT HAD AMERICA BEEN BLESSED WITH ISLAM

This speech was delivered on June 6, 1977 in the Hall of the Divinity College of Harvard University. The speaker was introduced to the audience by Mr. Mudassir Husain Siddiqui which included University teachers and scholars. A large number of students from different parts of the country also attended. The proceedings began with the recital of Sura-i-Wat-Teen by a Black American Muslim.

II

**Surely We created men of the best stature
Then We reduced him to the lowest of the low.**

—(XCV : 4-5)

Friends and Brothers,

Today I will begin my speech with the remark to which
I have been guided by the verses of the Quran that have just
been recited   These verses have shown me the path of speaking
to you   I am going to begin with something that may startle
you   The Western World which stretches from Europe to the
Americas is most fortunate, and yet it is most unfortunate.
Such a big contradiction, in the same breath, may seem strange
to you, but the verses which have been read to you, too, would
appear self-contradictory, though they convey a profound
reality. The same is the case with the whole of the West which,
for reasons to go into which will be unnecessary here, has been
vested by God with the leadership of the world. I have discussed
at length in my book, *Islam and the World*, how universal leadership came to pass into the hands of the West. So, as I have
said, what is true of man is, also, true of this part of the world.
It is, at once, lucky and unlucky. It would not have mattered
much had it been its own affair. Nations have risen to great
heights in the past, and, then, their decline has set in and they
have fallen into the abyss of obscurity. There would have been
no reason for us to pay a particular attention if it appertained
to a mere country.   But when that country is in the position of
leadership and its influence is felt throughout the world, it
assumes serious proportions.

America is fortunate because Nature has been most generous to it. The Lord has bestowed His gifts lavishly upon this country.   Its people are resourceful and enterprising.   They are full of enthusiasm for living.   They have been granted such a tenacity of purpose, resoluteness and pertinacity that they have made their country a paradise on earth. They have unravelled the mysteries of nature and harnessed its forces to their use.   In the words of Iqbal, they have ·"enchained the rays of the sun",. and "sought the orbits of the stars". They have turned the dust into gold. Now, in this land wealth pours down from the skies and rivers of milk and honey flow.   This is the result of the galvanic spirit, robust imagination and unflagging eagerness of the American people. The United States not only abounds in mineral resources, but has, also, the hands to exploit them. In this respect. it is exceedingly fortunate and the whole world is, as if it were, keenly desirous to prove it. Everyone is a beggar at its door, eager to solicit its favours.   But their ingenuity, sense of discipline and capacity for management, the people here have organised their life so well that the world at large is benefiting from it.   In the material and economic fields they are supreme.

You can justly be envious of America and admire it as much as you like.   I do not believe in partisanship whether religious, social or political. One must give praise where praise is due.

But. at the same time, this country is most unfortunate. I say it with a full sense of responsibility. Many of you may be shocked at it, but it is a fact.

He who enchained the sunbeams

It has been a tragedy not only for America but the whole of mankind that it concentrated entirely on material progress and made the physical world the sole sphere of its activity. It would have been a different story had it received correct guidance and the boon and blessing of true faith had reached it, and the Americans had, also, paid attention to morality with equal earnestness and enthusiasm and looked for the portents of God in *Anfas* i. e., within themselves, and not only in *Afaq* i. e., the horizons. If the intellectual faculties of the Americans had not been directed altogether towards finding a clue to the mysteries of nature and they, also, had cared to discover the secrets of the self—of the heart and the soul—, they would have realised that the world of heart was immeasurably more extensive than the world of matter, so much so that if the whole of the universe was dropped into the heart of man it would get lost like a pebble in an ocean. The people of America would, then, have been able to appreciate correctly the place of man in the grand design of creation. Of the time and energy they have recklessly spent on material sciences, and, as we all know, with what results, we have it in the Quran :

And   that   man   hath   only that for which he   maketh
effort,
And that his effort will be seen.
And   afterward he   will be   repaid   for   it   with   fullest
payment.
—(LIII : 39-41)
Each do We supply, both these and those, from the bounty
of thy Lord;
And   the   bounty   of   the   Lord   can   never   we walled   up.
—(XVII : 20)

Whatever field man chooses for himself, God will grant him success in it. Their is no limit to it; no thus far and no further. The consequences of the enterprise and industry of the West are before us. The world has shrunk and man has subjugated it for his own ends and interests. Had the Westerners exerted themselves, in the same way, on the heart, soul, and belief, the world would have known the true station of humanity. When the West worked on a tree, it produced from it a fruit no one could dream of. Identically, when it turned to Physics, Chemistry and Botany, it discovered new worlds. In the earlier days people were not inclined to believe in the plurality of the worlds and those who made such a claim were remorselessly punished by the Papal authority. But, today, a new world is being discoverd in almost everything. In the same way, had the West known the true station a humanity and appreciated the distinction God had conferred upon man, the history of our race would have been different.

Most appropriate religion

Two events were largely responsible for the tragedy which overtook not only the West, but the whole of mankind. One was the arrival of Christianity in the Western hemisphere. We, the Muslims, are, also, to blame and however much were we to regret it, it would not be unjustified. The fact is that the most appropriate religion for this part of the world would have been Islam which awakened the latent human capabilities, gave encouragement to intellect, and made man self-reliant and self-respecting. Says the Quran:

Surely We created man of the best stature. —(XCV : 4)
Verily We have honoured the children of Adam.
We carry them on the land and the sea, and have made provision of good things for them, and have preferred them over many of those whom We created with a marked preferment.   —(XVII : 70)
Lo ! I am about to place a viceroy in the earth.

—(II : 30)

Islam places the crown of Vicegerency on man's head than which there can be no greater honour. The whole structure of Islam is based upon the doctrine of Divine Unity and when it declares that man is *Khaleefat-ul-Laah* i. e., the Vicegerent of God on earth, it elevates him so much that one cannot think of a higher and nobler concept of humanity. Thus, in a Tradition, it is stated that on the Day of Judgement God will say to His bondsman, "I fell ill and you did not visit Me." The bondsman will reply, "Thou art the Lord of the Worlds. How could I visit Thee ?" God will, thereupon, say, "Did you not know that such and such a bondsman of Mine was ill and you did not care to visit him ? Had you gone to see him in order to comfort or help, you would have found Me with him."

God, again, will say, "O son of Adam ! I asked you for food, but you did not give it to Me." The bondsman will reply, "Thou art the Lord of the Worlds. How could I give Thee food ?" God will, then, say, "Are you not aware that such and such a bondsman of Mine begged you for food and you did not give it to him. Had you fed him you would have found it with Me." God, again, will say, "O son of Adam ! I was naked, but you did not cover Me with a garment." The bondsman will reply, "Thou art the Lord of the Worlds. How could I clothe Thee ?" God will, then, say, "Such and such a bondsman of Mine begged you for something to wear and you did not give it to him. Had you done that the dress would have reached Me."

What greater honour can there be for mankind ? Islam, further, tells that man is sinless by birth, his nature is pure, and his slate is clean. A Tradition has it that "every child is born on its nature i. e., pure and guiltless and it is its parents who make it a Jew, Chirstian or Fire-worshipper." They dye it in their own hue otherwise when a man is born he is on the *Colour of Allah.* Islam teaches that the innate characteristic, the fundamental reality of human nature is submission. There is no defect in it. It is basically sound. The Quran says : *It gets what it earns, and it suffers what it earns.* (II : 286)which means that it is beneficial for man what he earns and it is harmful for him what he earns with effort. The good deed a man does is in conformity with his nature while the wrong part he pursues is in defiance of it. The assertion that the good deeds of man are in response to his natural instincts whereas his misdeeds are, so to speak, a revolt against himself bears a most eloquent testimony to the inherent purity of human nature.

So, Islam was the most suitable religion for this land. Had a union taken place between the two, the history of mankind would have taken a different course. On the one side, there would have been the unbounded natural resources of America, the tremendous vitality, resoluteness and enterprise of its people— the will to forge ahead and to win new laurels, and, on the other, the moderation of Islam, its message of hope and confidence its incomparable quality of being the Faith of Nature and its insistance on the intrinsic innocence of man i. e., the doctrine that man is born free from sin and if he goes astray and falls into error, it is a passing phase and the rust that is formed on his heart as a result of it disappears as soon as he resolves to offer sincere repentance which is not a thing of constraint, but an inborn impulsion, and, that is why, a high place has been given to those who repent after sinning.

Islam gives encouragement to the creativeness of man and arouses his dorment capabilities. It is the faith of Monothism, of the Oneness of God. There is no speculative philosophy or empty idealism in it. It is based on solid facts and is such a simple religon that anyone can easily understand it. It does not put fetters on life, nor places obstacles in the path of knowledge, but elevates learning to an act of worship. It calls on man to study and reflect.

> And in earth are portents for those whose faith is sure, and (also) in yourselves. Can ye then not see ?
> —(LI : 20-21)

> (Who) reflect upon the creation of the heavens and the earth (and say) : Our Lord ! Thou createdst not this in vain.　　　　　—(III : 191)

> We shall show them Our portents on the horizons and within themselves.　　　　　—(XLI : 53)

Islam does not imprison the mind. On the contrary, it demands of man to make the fullest use of his mental faculties.

> And those who, when they are reminded of the revelations of their Lord, fall not deaf and blind thereat (but listen attentively and cogitate).　　　　　—(XXV : 73)

But, alas, the West opted out for a faith which upheld the doctrine of the Original Sin and gave rise to the worst kind of pessimism and frustration by hammering into man the belief that to sin was his destiny, and destiny was unalterable. Or, in other words, it was a hereditary trait with him, a congenital disease. It is a different matter that a man goes wrong and transgresses against a God-given law, but realises his mistake and makes amends for it. But if the idea is implanted in his mind that he is a born sinner, you can imagine to what abnormal reactions will he fall a prey.

Thus, one misfortune of this country was that it chose a religion which did not raise the stature of humanity, but put the mark of disgrace on its forehead and persuaded it to believe that it needed a personality that could redeem it by offering an atonement for its misdeeds. To make the matters worse, the inclination for monasticism and renunciation of the world soon appeared in the West.

The Church put impediments in the path of knowledge and understanding

The other calamity was that when the Church was in the ascendant, the ecclesiastics blocked the path of knowledge and investigation. At a time Europe was waking up and breaking the chains, the Papal authority stood before it like a thick wall and started measuring everything with its own yardstick. The Church opposed when it was claimed that the earth was round. Bruno, whose only crime was that he taught the plurality of the worlds, was declared a heretic and burnt alive, and Galileo another scientist of no less worth, was punished till he died in prison for having held that the earth moved round the sun. The Inquisition was established which performed its duty with such savage alacrity that the number of persons tried and punished by it was, in no way, less than the casualities in the last war.

The two things combined to turn the face of Europe decidedly towards materialism. The enlightened sections among the Europeans developed a strong aversion to everything associated with the ecclesiastics. They began to exhibit a definite intolerance of every kind of spiritual control. The feelings of disgust and disdain were directed not against a particular religion, but against the whole concept of religious belief and worship. In its haste, the West decided that no progress could be made until religion was discouraged and the bonds of salvery to the Church were broken.   Europe, thus, rose openly in revolt against the Church and set out on the journey of materialism, the mournful consequences of which stare us in the face everywhere.

Gentlemen, it is a long and painful story.   You all are educated people and you must have read about it.   Besides, the University at which I am speaking today is universally recognised as a great seat of learning.   I will, therefore, not go into the details.

Western Civilisation has completed its action

The Western Civilisation has reached the highest point of its development.   No one knows the mysteries of the universe save God, nor can anyone say, positively, what lies in store for us tomorrow. But, as the case is at present, this Civilisation has brought forth the best fruits it was capable of bearing.   Now, we are standing at the corss-roads of history.   The Western Civilisation has almost completed its action, and America, which is a major centre of it, is swaying merrily in the swing of its attainments.   It can proudly claim to have lifted every veil from the face of Nature and unfolded all its secrets—distances have been reduced and man is enjoying all the facilities he could think of.

Nevertheless, the heart of man is devoid of peace. His soul is unhappy. He has reached a stage where life seems meaningless. He is dazed and bewildered. What was needed at this juncture was that men were born in this very country who could pull it out of the morass of frustration and disillusionment, give it a new message and breathe a new life into it. The life is moving at a pace that has left man breathless. The modern Civilisation is taking him at break-neck speed, he knows not where. Neither the reins are his hands nor are his feet in the stirrups.

Ray of hope

I do not believe in the philosophy of chance happenings.   I feel that there is the Hand of God behind everything that takes place. *That is the Measuring of the Mighty, the Wise.* (XXXVI :37). You have come to live here in large numbers. There are not merely manual workers among you, but some highly gifted Muslims as well who are studying in the universities and engaged in valuable scientific investigation. Many of you have made your mark as scholars and researchists. What is more, Islam is spreading in America. It has made a dent. A number of Americans have either embraced Islam or are ready to do so. Our Black Muslim brethren are a source of strength to us. This country, in brief, seems to be taking a new turn and a new ray of hope is appearing. Due to our shortsightedness and internal dissensions we, in the past, lost the opportunity to come to its aid. Had Islam been propagated in Europe when the Ottomans had established their rule over a part of the Continent, or, even earlier, when the Moors had swept over Spain, the West, today, would not be finding itself in this predicament. It would not have been caught in the quagmire of materialism.

But, unfortunately, we did not rise to the occasion. How much do I wish that the Muslim evangelists had reached here when they had set out into the world in the early centuries of Islam. It is said that the Muslims had discovered America before Columbus. How wonderful it would have been had they taken advantage of it and given the message of Islam to the New World. But it was not to be, and the Islamic countries have been paying the penalty for the last two hundred years. I believe that the way the Muslim countries have, today. become the lackeys of the West and the treatment they are receiving at its hands is a punishment for the failure the of Muslims to convey to it the Message of God at the proper time.

But now the circumstances are taking a favourable course. Muslims are migrating to America, in a steady stream; from different lands and for different reasons. There is no Islamic country whose finest young men are not found here. Lastly, a large number of enterprising people are coming to it from the country where the House of Ka'aba is situated. You should, now, realise your responsibility which does not lie merely in acquiring higher education or solving your economic problem. You are not here only to earn and take back the money to your native lands and provide for your families. You should know that it is your duty to give this country what it lacks. If you look at its material attainments and scientific advancement, it presents a true picture of the Divine pronouncement, *Surely We created man of the best stature,* but if you think over its moral bankruptcy and the agony of its soul, you will find it at the level of *the lowest of the low.* Intellectual maturity and puerility exist side by side in America. On the one hand, the Americans are going to the moon, and, on the other. they are sinking into the lowest depths of moral degradation. The country that solved all the problems is finding itself helpless in providing a solution to the moral crisis of its youth. As Iqbal had said :

> He who enchained the sunbeams could not
> Unfurl the dawn on life's dark night.

I say it without hesitation that there is no Muslim country which can look the Westerners in the face and say : "See. it is here that you stumbled. With us is the panacea of your ills and the balm for your inner wounds. It is the Quran and the teachings of our Prophet." The bitter truth is that we have made ourselves unworthy of speaking to the West like men. We carry a heavy load of gratitude to it on our heads, and are immersed from head to foot in its favours. Our ignorance deposes against us. Our poverty shouts from the house-tops. Our arm is stretched out for alms. Such being the case, how can an Islamic country speak, like an equal, to the West which has the whip in hand and enjoys every kind of superiority—intellectual, political and economic ? Which Muslim country is there that can express the mildest criticism of the West or offer a suggestion ?

Your station is of men who invite to goodness

You may ascribe it to my imagination, but I will urge upon you to show them by your conduct and way of life that you have something to give to the West. You are not here simply to take, but are, also, capable of giving. No matter whether you are a University teacher or a student or working in a firm, you can prove the authenticity of Islam to those with whom you live or associate. You can arouse in them the feeling that Islam can still give them something. In spite of possessing everything, they are paupers; they are insolvent from within. They are not deriving the advantage they should be from their material achievements. The real furits of scientific and technological progress have been eluding them. You should have, first, faith in yourselves, in your station as the givers of the call to goodness. You are not mere gleaners to pick up the droppings. You can, also, fill their bowl with your own grain. It may sound preposterous in the present circumstances and many of my brothers and sisters may be wondering to what world do I belong.

But the Quran and the example of the Prophet fill me with faith and hope. The sacred Prophet had sent the following epistle to Caesar, who ruled over half of the then known world, when there was not enough to eat in his own house and the Muslim State had not been established in Medina.

In the Name of Allah, the Most Benevolent, the Most Merciful

From Mohammad, the bondsman and Messenger of Allah, to Heraclius, the Emperor of Rome.

Peace be upon him who follows the Guidance. I invite yon to the message of Islam. Accept Islam and you shall be delivered : two-fold will be Allah's reward to you. But if you turn away then on you will rest the sin of (the denial of) your community. Oh People of the Scripture ! Come to an agreement on a thing that is common between us and you : that we shall worship none but Allah, and ascribe no partner unto Him, and that none of us shall take others for lords beside Allah. And if you turn back upon it then bear witness that we are they who have surrendered (unto Him).

I am a follower of the Prophet who, with utmost self-reliance and trust in God, gave the call of Islam to the mightiest ruler of his time and in circumstances of utter poverty and powerlessness. When oven is not lighted in his house for months, when members of his household do not have a satisfactory meal even for two consecutive days, when his coffers are empty and his followers are few in number, he says to the Roman Emperor. "Accept Islam and you shall be delivered." We are the adherents of that Apostle. We must summon up courage to give to these people what they need, to make them realise that we possess what they are, regrettably, wanting in, and without which the Western Civilisation is doomed This Civilisation is ready to commit suicide. If anything can save it, it is the guidance of the Quran. A harmonious blending has to be worked out between material progress and spiritual values. Disaster awaits the world if materialism gains the upper hand over morality. This is the call our Islamic countries should give. They should tell plainly to the West, "Look here. You are drowning and we can save you." But is anyone of them in that position ? We have forfeited the right to do so. We are the hangers-on of the West. None of the Islamic countries has the courage to tell the West what ails its civilisation. They consider the Western Civilisation the last word in perfection. As someone has said, "The Qibla[1] of the world is *Haram*[2], and the *Qibla* of *Haram* is America." I make bold to say that, today, the Islamic countries and the Muslim ruling classes are incapable of giving any call to the West. But you can perform the duty by displaying self-confidence, by presenting before them a solid exemple of the Islamic way of life and by learning to be proud of your Faith. You should be grateful to the Lord for these favours. Through *Namaz*, supplication and freedom from servility to worldly ends and interests you should demonstrate to the world that materialism can never enslave your hearts and

1.   The place to which the Muslims turn in prayer.
2.   The holy K'aba in Mecca.

minds. You have not yet lost the ability to judge between good and evil. Worldly goods are not everything in your sight ; not even this existence. Hereafter is an article of faith with you. You hold as true that there is to come another life and another world at the end of this of mortal life. You believe that God is All-powerful, He has control over all things, and His good pleasure is the extreme limit of felicity and good fortune. God has given you the opportunity to acquaint the Americans with the realities that have receded into oblivion and Christianity has failed to revive them in spite of the vast resources at its disposal. You can discharge that responsibility, all your faults and weaknesses notwithstanding.

Friends ! I have taken a lot of your time. But you must make an allowance for the burning of my heart. Listen to the cry of anguish that rises from the depths of my soul. I can now attest before the Lord to have given the *Azan* in the biggest idol-hall of the world, and conveyed His Guidance to what can be the most appropriate place in the modern world. I shall deem myself successful if I have been able to evoke a sympathetic response in even one of my listeners here.

May Allah take from you, in an increasing degree, the service of his Faith and make you more useful to Islam and to this country than to yourselves, to your families, and to your native lands !

AMERICAN GENEROSITY IS BEING WASTED: THIS COUNTRY HAS NO SINCERE FRIENDS

This speech was delivered at the Islamic Centre of Washington on June 25, 1977. The invitation to it was given by Syed Mazhar Husain who also accompanied the speaker during the trip to Washington and introduced him to the audience. The meeting was attended, among others, by Indian, Pakistani and Arab scholars. The proceedings began with the recitation. by an Egyptian theologian of the section, *Set forth to them the parable of two men : For one of them We provided two gardens of grape-vines.........of Sura-i-Kahf* which was made the subject of his discourse by the Maulana.

III

Brothers and Sisters,

It makes me very happy to be with you here in Washington, the capital city of the United States of America, which may be described as the hub of the world. Today its influence is felt everywhere, and in all spheres of life, social, political and economic. We may like it or not, but no one can deny it.

What is lacking here ?

How did America acquire that position and what part has the skill, industry, unity of interests and capacity to organise and act jointly with one another of the American people, and their scientific, industrial and technological progress played in it, and how much of it is due to our own negligence and short-comings is a very complex question, and, I am sure, you will agree that it will be out of place to try to discuss it here. Thinkers, political scientists and historians have analysed it from various angles and offered their explanations.

From the material point of view, this country is a paradise on earth, and, excuse me, this is what has brought you to it from your native lands, India, Pakistan, Syria, Egypt, Saudi Arabia. and, so on. There is no harm in it either, for don't the pieces of iron collect around the magnet or the thirsty people rush to the place where water is found ? I have seen America from coast to coast, both as an ordinary tourist and a student of the Quran and history, and the thing I have found wanting here is exactly what has been alluded to in the Quranic Verses we have just heard.

May God bless the learned friend who recited the verses from *Sura-i-Kahf* and reward him bounteously in both the worlds. He has brought us face to face with a world of truths and realities, and, at least, rendered a great service to me. I was wondering what I was going to say at this meeting. There are, of course, so many things one can talk about, but the difficulty lies in the choice. I was thinking what message could I deliver to you in the States, what would you like to hear from me that, suddenly, the Quran came to my rescue as it always does, and I felt that a wonderful portrait of the Modern Age, which had reached the pinnacle of material development, had been drawn in these verses.

For one of them We provided two gardens of grape-vines. Both the gardens gave their fruit and withheld naught thereof. And We caused a river to gush forth therein. And he had fruit. And he said unto his comrade, when he spoke with him : I am more than thee in wealth and stronger in respect of men.

—(XVIII : 33-35)

Can a better portrait be possible of modern America? *Gardens of grape-vines* ! Take any part of this great land and does it not present a spectacle of luxuriance and plentitude ? What is lacking in it ? What fruit is not found here ? All the gifts of the Lord are abundantly available in this country. Still there is something that is sadly wanting and to which attention has been drawn by the thoughtful and believing friend in these words :

When thou entered the garden, why did thou not say : That which Allah willeth (will come to pass) ! There is no strength save in Allah !

—(XVIII : 40)

Only *Masha Allah, laa quwata illa billaah* (that which Allah willeth : there is no power but in God) is missing. This *Masha Allah, laa quwata illa billaah* can turn the dust into gold, elevate materialism into worship of the highest order, and tame the rebellious horse of the carnal self so that it became a blessed mode of transport for taking man to his destination. It is the master-key that can open any lock. If the Western World does not possess anything, it is this. On the face of it, these are just a few words which we utter frequently in everyday life. *Masha Allah*, when did you come? *Masha Allah*, when you had this new suit made? And, so on.

In fact, we have lost appreciation of the ocean of eloquence and profundity that is contained in this short, pithy expression and the marvellous power it possesses of subduing the materialistic aspirations and conceit of man that lead him into the deception that whatever is happening around him is of his own choice and making. That is why, we utter it mechanically, without the faintest idea of its intrinsic significance. What *Masha Allah* denotes, in sum, is that whatever takes place in the world is at the command of God and by His power and authority; the credit for it does not go to man, nor does praise belong to him.

Praise be to Allah, Lord of the Worlds.

—(I : 1)

And :

But His command, when He intendeth a thing, is only that He saith unto it : Be ! and. it is.

—(XXXVI : 81)

What has been set forth in the two aforementioned verses and the supremeness that has been affirmed in *Allah is He who raised the heavens without any pillars*, (XIII : 2) have got compressed into the single phrase of *Masha Allah, laa quwata illa billaah*. Only that which Allah willeth will happen. He is the Author of all things, the Creator of all things. There is no power save in Allah.

Today, America is a living example of *He hath loaded you with His favours both without and within*, (XXXI : 20), *and Abundantly supplied with sustenance from every place*. (XVI : 112). Wealth is springing here from the earth and pouring down from the heavens. Then, why is it not giving the message of peace, good understanding and security to the world ?

America has no sincere friends

The United States can claim to be the benefactor of the world, and, may God forbid, with many people it is the Great Provider of the daily bread. But how many countries feel sincerely grateful to it? America is giving food, money and arms to scores of nations and aiding them in the implementation of their development plans. But what is it getting in return ?

A number of countries feel protected against external aggression because of their defence pacts and other arrangements with America. For them its friendship is the greatest guarantee of peace and the preservation of their sovereignty. Yet, no one is giving thanks to it. On the countrary, they never miss an opportunity to denounce it. An undercurrent of hatred is found everywhere against it. America has no sincere friend, no true well-wisher in any part of the world.

Do the leaders of this great country not feel it? Are its thinkers blissfully unaware of this reality ? No, they must be knowing that for all its dollars what America is getting back is a kick here and a let-down there. But have they ever cared to go to the root of the matter? If they do a little self-introspection, they will find that at the base of it all lies America's own insincerity. Its entire concept and mechanism of aid and assistance is devoid of earnestness. Its generosity is a cloak for the exploitation of the weaker and the poorer nations. It gives, but not to enable them to stand on their feet. Its magnanimity is aimed at the perpetuation of their dependence upon it.

The Apostles and their followers served mankind with sincerity and they came to be loved

The Prophets devoted their time and energy to the service of mankind and gave it the priceless gifts of faith, truth, sincerity and universal brotherhood, and, as a consequence of it, nations and communities became their slaves. The Egyptians,

Syrians and Iraqis renounced their languages, cultures and ancient civilisations, and willingly accepted the rule of the Arabs, or, rather, of the Muslim Arabs, and even their tongue. Nowadays, a campaign is being carried on in our Eastern countries against the English language, so much so that it is being erased from the sign-boards, but so far not a voice has been raised against the Arabic language in the Arab World. In fact, no reaction or hostility against the Islamic Civilisation or the Arab-Islamic culture is felt in the Arabic-speaking countries while, perhaps, a feeling of digest and intolerance is building up against the European Civilisation in various parts of the world and the day is not far off when they will throw it out and revive the Eastern or their own indigenous civilisations.

America is unblest with true Faith

There is everything in America save the effulgence of the Book of God and Divine Guidance. The belief that it is God who is directing the affairs of the world, He has power over all things and all that we have achieved is by His grace and we should spend what we possess according to his Will and Command and in His path is not to be found in this mighty land. If anything is wanting here, it is this.

It has *Gardens of grape-vines*, but not *Masha Allah laa quwata illa billaah*, and the owner of the earthly paradise can only be he who has been indicated in the Quran. In the parable of two men, the possessor of the gardens is a plain materialist, a rebel, an ungrateful soul, and an egotist while the other is a truthful Believer : he is weak, he does not possess *Gardens of grape-vines*, but he is a Believer and God has blessed him with faith.

Both the *Gardens* withheld nothing. They poured out all that they had, like a spring gushing forth from the earth. Abundant was their produce.

Now, the turn of the other brother comes. He says, "Very well, but why did you not say : *That which Allah Willeth will come to pass; there is no power save in Allah*, when you went into the garden? You should have avowed that it all was by the grace and benevolence of the Lord, and a manifestation of His Might and Mercifulness."

Had America been religious-minded

America is not saying that all this is the gift of God. But why ? It is a long and distressing story, and, also, shameful for you and me. It is long because it goes back to hundreds of years; distressing because had it been otherwise, had America been blessed with the wealth of faith and had it been religious-minded, the world would have been presenting another picture, the history of mankind would have been different, the danger of war would not have been hovering over our heads and the nuclear energy would not have been causing fear and suspicion in the minds of men; and shameful because we, the Muslims, failed in our duty to carry Islam to this part of the world. The Lord gave us many opportunities. Muslims came to this land when it had begun to raise its head like an infant; all the portents were there of its enormous potentialities, but we were caught in deep slumber; and even before that when we ruled over Spain we should have striven to instill the message of Islam into the heart and soul of Europe instead of building Al-Hamara and Al-Zehra and erecting stately mansions and magnificient mosques, and the evangelists and preachers of Islam should have spread over the Continent. But is was not to be. Hence I say that the story is, also, shameful. However, what was to happen has happened. If this country needs anything now it is that a living bond is forged between it and Apostleship. But Christianity cannot do that.

Failure of Christianity

Christianity had proved its powerlessness a long time ago. If you read the history of Christianity you will find that either it was not content with anything less than monasticism or there was so much of stagnation and prejudice in it that it felt compelled to push back the rising tide of knowledge and critical investigation. Christianity was not equipped to lend guidance to this great land. It did not possess the strength to show the path of moderation and comprehensiveness to the eager, ardent and enterprising peoples of Europe and America. It could not say, *Show us the Straight path; or Our Lord Give us good in this world, and good in the Hereafter.* Christianity was not willing to say : *Our Lord ! Give us good in this world......*because it believed in the renunciation of the world.

Islam is the religion of balanced and comprehensive teachings

It was left to our precursors to tell that they, alone, could do so. Now, it is our duty to present such a balanced and comprehensive image of Islam that the people of the West realised that it, alone, could lead them along the right path. If the bond is established between America and Islam, the doors of Divine Mercy and Benevolence will open for the whole world, the clouds of war will disperse, hatred will disappear from the hearts, and man will cease to be a hunter of man : he will become a man in the true sense of the word, and live only as an enemy of Satan. This only Islam can do, and whenever it is going to happen in America, it will be through Islam.

Christianity had lost its soul centuries ago when it had stepped out of Palestine and made its way into the Roman Empire. I feel proud to say it here in America which is the most powerful country in the world, today, that Christianity, as it is, is not the religion of the Apostle who had been raised up by God with the message of peace and love. It is the creation of St. Paul and the product of his ingenuity. It is the Christianity of St. Paul, and of the Middle Ages, and it would be futile to expect it to guide the steps of a dynamic country like the United States or an impatient generation like the present one. It possesses neither a comprehensive programme of life nor the moral strength to uphold the values related to the inner existence of man.

A word to the Americans

Oh, citizens of the United States ! My best wishes to you. I don't grudge you your attainments. I don't look at your progress with contempt. What I ask you most earnestly is only to add *Masha Allah, wa laa quwata illa-billaah* to what you have. Subordinate your worldly possessions and phenomenal achievements to the will of God. Place it all under the control and authority of the Divine law. Use it for the rebirth and redemption of mankind and the generation of an atmosphere of equality, fraternity, justice and freedom from fear in the world. Let there be no distinctions of race, colour or wealth between man and man. Use your enormous resources for reconstruction of the world. You will, thus, be helping yourselves as well for, without it, your civilisation cannot survive. Its days are numbered. As Iqbal has put it

> The arrant intellect that laid bare the treasures of
> nature,
> In its own nest is threatened by the lightning it has
> released.

Deliver the message of Islam

The Muslims, on the contrary, are fortunate to have been blessed with a unique comprehensiveness. They realise the worth and singificance of this world, but, at the same time, regard it only a transitional stage in man's onward journey. With them the real and permanent abode is the Hereafter. Their attitude towards life is governed by the Quranic verse which says :

> And for that Abode of the Hereafter We assign it unto those who seek not oppression in the earth, nor yet corruption. The (good) sequel is for those who ward off (evil).

> —(XXVIII:83)

In the end, I thank you that you come here out of love for a Muslim brother and gave him a patient hearing. May Allah protect you and your faith, and your next generation, also, be a believer in Islam.

Die not die save as Muslims.

—(II :132)

My fervent prayer is that you remained true to this commandment.

May you be bowing your heads low before God, offering up *Namaz* regularly and adhering steadfastly to the *Kalima* as long as you live in this world, and when you depart from it, the radiance of Faith may be in your hearts and the *Kalima* of *Laa ilaaha illallaah, Mohammadur rasulullaah* on your lips !

PART TWO

MUSLIM IMMIGRANTS IN AMERICA

★ HOPES ★ FEARS ★ SUGGESTIONS

THE PLACE OF A MUSLIM— AND HIS MESSAGE

Being the Friday sermon delivered on June 3, 1977 in the assembly room of the United Nations where the employees of the Muslim and Arab countries meet for the Friday service, a large number of Arabs participated in the congregation among whom responsible members of the staffs of Rabita-i-Aalam-i-Islami and the United Nations were prominent.

IV

You are the hunter of the Phoenix; it is only the
beginning,
The world of fish and fowl has not been created in
vain.

The Quran says :

So lose not heart, nor fall into despair, for ye must
gain mastery if ye are true in Faith.   (—III : 139)

This verse was revealed at a time when Islam was in its
infancy, and the Islamic State had not been founded. The
light of Faith had, till then, not spread beyond the Peninsula of
Arabia, and Arabs were leading a life of intense poverty and
indigence. They, generally, ate dates, the flesh of a camel and
barley-bread, wore rough and coarse clothes and lived in mud-
huts or ordinary tents. The state of misery and helplessness in
which the Arabs passed their days has been described in these
words by the Quran than which there can be no better and
more trustworthy testimony

And remember, when you were few and reckoned
feeble in the land and were in fear lest men should extir-
pate you.

(—VIII : 26)

Such was the condition of the Arabs. As against it, the
Romans and the Iranians enjoyed the monopoly of leadership
in the world. They had built up magnificent civilisations and
their writ ran over a vast segment of humanity. The two Powers

had divided the Eastern and Western parts of the civilised world between themselves : the Iranians ruled over the Eastern part while the Western part was under the domination of the Romans. They wallowed in wealth and all the good things of life were available to them in plenty.

It was in these circumstances that the Quran challenged the power-drunk nations of Rome and Iran and instilled the spirit of dignity and self-confidence into the weak and helpless Arab Muslims. It declared :

So lose not heart, nor fall into despair; for ye must gain mastery if ye are true in Faith.   (—III : 139)

The Quran challenged the Quraish of Mecca and the Romans and Persians, and, then, for the comfort and solace of the leader and guide of the handful of Muslims, the Prophet Mohammad (Peace and Blessings of the Lord be on him), *Sura-i-Yusuf* was revealed.   The Quran proclaimed :

For those who question, for them are signs (of Allah's sovereignty) in the life-story of Yusuf (Joseph) and his brothers.   (—XII : 7)

The *Sura* was brought to an end with these words :

Till, when the Messengers despaired and thought that they were denied, then came unto them Our help, and whom We would was saved. And Our wrath cannot be warded from the guilty.

In their history, verily, there is a lesson for men of understanding. It is no invented story but (the Quran is) a confirmation of the existing (Scripture) and a detailed explanation of everything and a guidance and a mercy for those who believe. (—XII : 110-111)

Similarly, the voice of *Sura-i-Qasas* thundered in the world. The Lord revealed the *Sura* in an atmosphere of oppression and fear.

Ta. Sin. Mim. These are revelations of the Scripture that maketh plain. We narrate unto thee (somewhat) of the story of Moses and Pharaoh with truth, for folk who believe.

Lo ! Pharaoh exalted himself in the earth and made its people castes. A tribe among them he oppressed, killing their sons and sparing their women. Lo ! he was of those who work corruption.

And We deemed to show favour unto those who were oppressed in the earth and to make them examples and to make them the inheritors. And to establish them in the earth, and to show Pharaoh and Haman and their hosts that which they feared from them.   (—XXVIII : 1-6)

Who could have dreamt of the good in those dreadful conditions ? Who could prophesise that the destitute and empty-handed, oppressed and down-trodden Muslims would shine on the firmament of history ? No wise or sensible person, gifted with any amount of foresight could say to those handful of men : *So lose not heart, nor fall into despair ; for ye must gain mastery if ye are true in Faith.*

But this announcement had filled the hearts of Muslims with such courage and enthusiasm that the mighty Romans and Persians appeared to them to be no more than pygmies. To quote the Quran once again :

And when thou seest them their figures please thee; and if they speak thou givest ear unto their speech. (But in fact, they are) as though they were propped up blocks of wood.   (—LXIII : 4)

When the helpless Arabs came out of their desert land, endued with the wealth of Faith, they cared nothing for the strength and vastness of Roman and Persian Empires and swept over them like an irresistible tidal-wave. In the words of Iqbal :

Desert and oceans fold up at their kick,
And mountains shrink into mustard-seeds.
Indifferent to the riches of the world it makes,
What a curious thing is the joy of love ?

Judged by the law of cause and effect, the Arabs, or rather, the whole of mankind were caught between the two jaws of a lion. When the Arabs ventured forth, they were a new power, a supernatural power. They were now a unique people fired with a singular passion. They were, of course, weak and poor. No part of the earth was under their rule. But when they stepped out of Arabia, intoxicated with the wine of Monotheism, they began to understand the difference between man and man, Faith and Infidelity, and form and reality, and the contrast between the 'Fountain of Immortality' and the 'Mirage of the Desert' become clear to them. God had endowed them with the light of Faith, and, in the twinkling of an eye, they gained a full mental and spiritual grasp of the nature and singificance of man's destiny. To eat, drink and be merry was not the high aim and purpose of his creation. His destiny lay in : *Surely We created man of the best stature*. When the Muslims had comprehended this fundamental truth, and the reality of the world and what lay beyond it had become clear to them, false manifestations of worldly power and glory failed to impress them and the ass dressed in the tiger's skin began to look to them the ass that it was. Caesar and Chosroes were, now, no more to them then the birds chattering in a cage : the cage, was marvellous—it was made of gold, but a cage, after all, even if it was studded with diamonds and was very extensive and there were ponds and orchards and stately buildings in it. The Arabs saw those who wore crowns on their heads or were known by the dignified denominations of ministers, army generals, princes and philosophers with an eye with which the performers in a play are seen and they refused to be over-awed by them. They knew that their hearts were frozen, their souls were dead and their minds had become sterile, and they strove to hide their inner insolvency in vulgar ostentation and in the sycophancy of servile flatterers. The Arabs realised that they were mere human figures, devoid of the force of will and the strength of purpose, and their thoughts and activities were directed solely towards the appeasement of the senses. They had no higher aim or ideal in life. There was no place for human sympathy in their calculations. Men were only the tools for the realisation of their desires and ambitions.

There were crowns on their heads, but the heads were empty, and costly dresses on their bodies, but the bodies were strengthless.

When the Arabs set out as the redeemers of humanity and with the object of rescuing it from savagery and barbarism that had been going on for centuries, the reality I have indicated dawned upon them. When they set out to deliver men from the bondage of fellow-men to the bondage of One God, from the narrowness of the world to its extensiveness, and from the injustice of their faiths and creeds to the fairness of Islam. the soul-less pomp and splendour seemed worthless to them and the powerful empires no more than a toy-house. To lower the flags of the Romans and Persians was a child's play to them.

The Quran had filled the illiterate and backward Arabs with ardour and strength. It had infused their cold and vacant hearts with pride, self-confidence and magnanimity. It had taught them the properties of things, their essential qualities and effects. They came out armed and enriched with these truths and snbjugated the world, but not to rule over it as other races had done. They had set out to make the mankind that had gone astray to bow its head before One God and to bring it under the shadow of Islamic justice and equity.

Gentlemen, We are meeting, today. at the headquarters of the United Nations. Now that we are representing numerous states and governments, we are more worthy of the dignity and self-reliance that was enjoyed by the early Arab Muslims. We deserve more to be addressed by the heavenly voice by which they had been addressed : *So lose not heart, nor fall into despair; for ye must gain mastery if ye are true in Faith.*

When this verse was revealed, there was no government of the Arabs in any part of the world; there was not a government even in the Peninsula of Arabia; Islam had made its advent barely ten years ago and it was toddling like a child. But if God found them worthy of being addressed with those soul-stirring words, do we not merit to be the recipients of that Divine edict today, when we represent forty states and a large number of our flags are flying on the building of the United Nations ? Though we do not possess nuclear arsenals and are lagging behind in scientific knowledge and modern education and do not come up to the standard the Western nations due to our apathy and internal discord and failure to appreciate the true worth of the Islamic teachings, we are definitely in a better shape than the Arabs of the earliest decades of Islam who did not have even a state or government of their own. Don't we, then, also deserve to be told : *So lose not heart, nor fall into despair : for ye must gain mastery if ye are true in Faith.*

This conviction is the real price of a truthful Believer. It is the cell without which a torch is worthless. This belief is the make-weight that brings down the scale of a balance in which it is put. It is the same make-weight that had been put in the balance by the sacred Prophet in the form of these memorable words in the thick of the Battle of Badr :

> Oh Lord ! If these handful of men are killed today, Thou shalt not be worshipped on the earth till the end of time.

The holy Prophet had realised that it was the time for repentance and supplication ; God had endued him with wisdom and understanding, discernment and good judgement. There was no future for Islam and Muslims if the outcome of the Battle of Badr was going to be determined by numbers and plain strength. They would have been wiped out from the face of the earth for there were only three hundred and thirteen Muslims while against them was arrayed an army, 1000 strong and fully equipped. How could the small band of Muslims privail over the mighty horde of the Pagans ? At that critical hour, the Prophet turned to God with earnest repentance and prayer and entreated Him in these historic words :

> If these handful of man are killed today, Thou shalt not be worshipped on the earth till the Day of the Last Judgement.

This is our worth and station. The Islamic countries carry a weight in the world and even in the United Nations. Were the people whom we have the honour to represent possessed of a living faith, permeating every nerve and fibre of their existence, the Muslims would even now be honourable in the world and commanding a position of strength and importance.

Brothers, do not look up to anyone for aid or support, Avoid being a hanger-on of others. Borrowed strength is ephemeral. It does no endure. Also let it not be that your name was shone in the comity of nations, and. numerically, you were strong in the population count of the world, but had no weight in the scales of God. We can be weighty in the scales of God only when we are truthful Believers, the spark of Faith is present in our hearts and we are not only the bearers of the message of Islam. but also proud of it, even here in the United States. the citadel of Western power, and can say on the trumpet's tune that we are Muslims and proud of Islam and that we are an imperishable people and the custodians of the Divine message. We are no parasites or spongers. but possess our own culture and civilisation and we are not going to accept any grafting upon it. The Lord has bestowed the greatest boon and blessing upon us which is Islam.

God will be our Helper and Protector when we are proud of Islam, and Islam is ours and we are of and for Islam. It is the promise of the Almighty, and Allah never breaks His promise. Says the Quran :

If ye help (in the cause of) Allah, He will help you and plant your feet firmly.   (—XLVII : 7)

But it we remain Muslims only in name and the reality of Islam is not present in us. we cannot hope for any help from the Lord since it is Faith alone that counts with Him and carries weight.

May Allah grant us the good fortune to revive the Islamic values in our midst and to cherish them again : to bend only before Him, and fear no one aside of Him, and be loyal to His faith. and proud of His message ! We beseech Him from the depths of our hearts to confer this wealth upon us. He, indeed, is able to do all things.

BEWARE OF THE EMERGENEC OF A EUROPEAN OR AMERICAN ISLAM

This speech was delivered at the Islamic Centre of New Jersey on June 4, 1977. Introducing the speaker, the Egyptian scholar, Dr. Sulaiman Duniya eulogised the services of Indian Muslims to the Arabic language and Islamic sciences and said that non-Arab Muslims had taken an equal part in the propagation and preservation of Islam with the Arabs, if not greater. He, also stressed the universal character of Islam, claiming that it transcended geographical and political boundaries.

V

Friends and Brothers,

It is my good fortune to meet you at this great Islamic Centre, This is my first visit to North America. Before it, I used to read and hear about this land and the progress Islam was making in it. I had, also, some knowledge of the religious inclination and solicitude of the Muslims who had taken up residence here. But I did not imagine that I would be meeting so many of my religious brethren in this far-off country or witnessing such a keen interest and enthusiasm for Islam.

On coming here I realised that Islam was trying to obtain a foothold in the United States which enjoyed the position of leadership in the contemporary world owing, largely, to its phenomenal advances in the fields of science and industry. By the grace of God, Islam has made its debut in this part of the world and is making a steady headway, and, God willing, the day is not far when an Islamic society will be established here.

It is, of course, a good augury for Islam and a matter of joy for the Muslims, but I, also, have some misgivings by reason of what little knowledge I possess of history. The establishment of an Islamic society so far away from the centres of Islamic faith and civilisation is open to grave risks and can lead to catastrophic consequences. Dr. Sulaiman Duniya, from whose writings I, too, have profited, has very aptly remarked that Islam is not exclusive to any country. I wholly agree that Islam is not a territorial faith, yet, it also needs a distinctive environment, a congenial climate, and a predisposition that may transcend presonal, cultural and intellectual standards and give forth, as one would say, the aroma of Islam. It requires an Islamic homeland for it is neither a mystical doctrine nor a philosophy nor a collection of soulless beliefs and rituals, but a real, living and all-embracing faith.

Islam, at once, is comprehensive of Idea and Action, Morality and Monetary Dealings, and Emotion and Intellect. In the same way, it, also, is a special kind of natural inclination and a peculiar state of mind. It embraces all the manifold aspects of human personality—spiritual and material, moral and physical, emotional and intellectual, and personal and social. It casts a man into a new mould. Whoever embraces Islam with an open heart believing it to be the chosen faith of the Lord and the Last of the Divine Messages will get cast into the mould of Islam. He will be transformed so radically as if he had been born anew because Islam is a complete and eternal plan of life which comprehends all the aspects of change and revolution and perfection and beauty. Islam is not a wooden dogma or a traditional religion. but a faith that permeates through the inmost recesses of the heart and soul.

If the true image of Islam is present before the mind's eye, it would be evident that it is not something that can, simply, be transmitted through the written or spoken word or seen in the books, but a typical way of thought. and a distinctive state of feeling. Hence it passes judgement about the goodness and badness, desirability and undesirability of things, as is related about the holy Prophet that he liked or disliked many things. He, for example, liked to begin every good act with the right hand so much so that be started combing his hair from the right side or when he wore the shoes, he began with the right foot. Similarly, there were many things that gave him pleasure or made him annoyed and uncomfortable. Islam, in fact, is an Apostolic of empyreal way of life that has come down from the heaven of heavens and the Divine Messengers have been its bearers and custodians, and they have left it behind as their legacy.

This is why, God had described Islam as *Sibghatullah* (Colour of Allah). Were it only a body of doctrines or a code of conduct it would not have been called *Sibghat* which denotes a 'mark', a 'colouring', and a 'distinguishing feature'. This can be possible only when Islam draws a clear line of demarcation between one man and another, between one life, character and temperament, and another life, character and temperament, and brings out clearly the difference among the standards of things and values of life. The criterion of Islam is quite different from the criterion of Infidelity. Hence, you will find warnings in the compilations of the Traditions and Sunnah of the Prophet against the Age of Ignorance and its practices. For instance, sometimes, it is said about a thing that it is a practice of the Age of Ignorance, and, sometimes, that is very much like the zealotry and arrogance of those days. It is set forth in the Quran;

(O ye women); Bedizen not yourselves with the bedizenment of the Time of Ignorance.

(—XXXIII : 33)

But why ? The Age of Ignorance having ended long ago, for what purpose did the Quran call upon men to shun it ? It was because Ignorance was a definite way of life and had its own values and standards for judging the goodness and badness, lawfulness and unlawfullness of things, and it was a way of life which the Lord viewed with disfavour. It is mentioned in the Traditions that "God looked at the earth and was displeased with the Arabs and non-Arabs who dwelt on it except for a few People of the Scripture".

The Almighty disliked Ignorance; He cursed it, and declared it undesirable for the bondmen. Hence, it was said : *Bedizen not yourselves with the bedizenment of the Time of Ignorance.* And, also :

When the unbelievers got up in their hearts heat and

cant : the heat and cant of Ignorance.

(—XLVIII : 26)

Whenever the sacred Prophet noticed a trait of Ignorance in a Muslim. he took exception to it, saying : "You are still under the influence of Ignorance'. For instance, when he saw an illustrious Companion like Abu Zarr Ghifari ill-treating his slave and beating him up, the Prophet observed : ··The inclination towards Ignorance has not yet gone out of you". The worthy Companion, on his part, was so deeply affected by the rebuke that he, at once, started treating his slave like an equal and gave him to eat and wear what he ate and wore himself.

Had Islam not been possessing a distinctive character and temperament, the Lord would not have used the word, *Colour*, in respect of it.

The Colour of Allah : and who is better than Allah at Colouring.

(—II : 138)

Exhorting, further, the bondmen to follow the Apostles, the Lord proclaimed, giving out a long and lustrous list of Divine Messengers :

And We bestowed upon him Issac and Jacob; each of them We guided; and Noah did We guide aforetime; and of his seed (We guided) David and Solomon and Job and Joseph and Moses and Aaron. Thus do We reward the good.

And Zachariah and John and Jesus and Elias. Each one (of them) was of the righteous.

And Ishmael and Elisha and Jonah and Lot. Each one of them did We prefer above (Our) creatures, with some of their forefathers and their offspring and their brethren; and We chose them and guided them unto a Straight Path. Such is the guidance of Allah wherewith He guideth whom He will of His bondmen. But if they set up (for worship) aught beside Him, all that they did would have been in vain.

(—VI : 85-89)

And, again :

Those are they whom Alllah guideth, so follow their guidance.

(—VI : 91)

Afterwards, the Lord determined that the command was exclusively with regard to the Prophet Mohammad whose life was a perfect model for mankind and an ideal example. The following words were thus, addressed to the Believers through the holy Prophet

Say, (O Mohammad, to mankind); If you love Allah, follow me; Allah will love you and forgive you your sins.

(—III : 31)

Islam is more sensitive than any other faith. It is enough for a man to call himself a Christian, and, after it, he can adopt whatever social, cultural or intellectual standards he likes. A friend of mine once said to an educated Hindu gentleman, "My brother, if a Muslim is asked who is a Muslim, he unhesitatingly replies that whoever recites and believes in the holy Kalima of *Laa Ilaaha Illallaah, Mohammadur rasulullaah* (There is no deity save One God. and Mohammad is His Apostle) is a Muslim. This affirmation sums up the whole of Islam. Now, what will your answer be if the same question was put to you concerning a Hindu ? I do not want a long and exhaustive reply because there are enough books in my library by the help of which one can understand the Brahmin or Vedantic philosophy. I have only a few minutes to spare and I want you to explain Hinduism quickly". My friend related that the Hindu gentleman paused for a while, and, then, said : "A Hindu can believe or refuse to believe in any-thing. If a person calls himself a Hindu, he is a Hindu, and, after it, it does not matter what he believes in or rejects. He remains a Hindu".

But it is not the same with Islam. As I have said, it is a highly sensitive faith and is more quickly affected by things that are inimical to it than any other religion. Its limits are marked out very clearly. It leaves no one in doubt about itself. In concrete, well-defined and clear-cut terms it makes it known that this is Islam and this is Infidelity; this is Islam and this is Ignorance; this is lawful and this is forbidden; and this is where Islam ends and Infidelity and Apostasy begin. Such an explicit concept of Apostasy, perhaps, does not exist in any other faith. In Islam, to be an Apostate is a mortal sin, the very thought of which makes the hair stand on end. It is stated in a Tradition that ''the sign of perfection in faith is that the idea of going back to Apostasy, after a man has embraced Islam, is as repugnant to him as being thrown into the fire.''

When such is the disposition of Islam, the responsibility of the Muslims who are settled in Europe or America becomes much greater. Had Islam, like the other faiths, been only a body of beliefs and practices, it would have been different, but if it is a *Colour* and a programme of life, and stands, also, for a state of feeling and awareness, and is much more sensitive than the other religions as well, and calls for a fundamental change in the values and ideals of things, the matter becomes far more complex.

We can, therefore, not rest content with reading books and treatises, however, weighty they may be. Books, of course, are necessary but we cannot cultivate the Islamic spirit wholly through them, nor develop the Islamic mood and temperament. Our real need is an Islamic region, an Islamic *Colouring* and an Islamic environment in which we can see, hear and feel Islam directly. Personal contacts; social intercourse and the adoption of the Islamic mode of living are its essential conditions. We should go to places where the Islamic way of life and Islamic society are present in any measure and we can have some experience of Islam as a living force.

For this reason, the company of Muslims and truthful Believers is necessary to the extent that God felt the need to tell the sacred Prophet, whose life was a model of perfection, to seek the company of pious and warmly devoted bondmen.

Restrain thyself along with those who cry unto their Lord at morn and evening seeking His countenance; and let not thine eyes overlook them, desiring the pomp of the life of the world; and obey not whose heart We have made heedless of Our remembrance, who followeth his own lust and whose case hath been abandoned.

(—XVIII : 28)

When such was the case with the sacred Apostle we can imagine how important it would be for common Muslims like us to spend some time with the truthful and the pure in heart.

Oh ye who believe ! Be careful of your duty to Allah, and be with the truthful.

(—IX : 119)

The Islamic society here being in the initial stages of evolution, we must not neglect our duty towards it. I am confident that, by the grace of God, this infant society will not only endure but, also, flourish and attain maturity and the means and opportunities of training and discipline will be available to it which are nothing but faith and belief, study and investigation, learning and culture, and good company and exertion. Those who make sincere efforts for the glory of the Divine Faith, for them the Lord opens the doors of wisdom, faith and discernment that are beyond human imagination.

And for those who strive in Us, We surely guide them to Our paths, and lo, Allah is with the good.

(—XXIX : 69)

Such, in brief, are the responsibilites you owe to the society you have founded in this country. It would never have come into existence had you not migrated to America and taken up residence here. Now, with it, you should, also, take pains to assure that it develops into an ideal Islamic society and does not remain confined to the ideological sphere alone because, as we know, Islam is not merely a social, political or economic concept, but before all this, it is an indivisible and indissoluble creed that permeates the whole existence. It is a state of mind and a design of life. The Islam of the holy Companions possessed all these attributes. They were Muslims by all standards, spiritual, moral and practical, and criterion for all things. Hence, it was said by Abdullah bin Masud that "what the Muslims consider good is good, also, in the judgement of God". According to the authorities, the word 'Muslims' here denotes the Companions. It will, thus, mean that what the Companions hold to be good is good also in the sight of the Lord and what they, collectively, regard bad is bad.

Islam and the Quran demand of the Muslims to be the criterion of truth and virtue. They should possess a genuine Islamic disposition so that the Americans, here, can see distinctly the difference between their own society which is being driven mercilessly by Materialism and the Islamic society that is pure, healthy and dignified—a society which spends its nights in prayer and repentance and days in seeking honest sustenance and rendering selfless service to mankind.

The creation of such a society will, positively, lead to the victory of Islam. On seeing it, the American will exclaim that the real joy of living is in the Islamic society and not in his own, and advance towards it instinctively and curse the stinking environment in which he has been brought up.

I fear the day, in America as elsewhere, when we will withdraw into our shells and get entangled in the labyrinth of study and research, and our connecting links with the real fountainhead of Islam and with the Islamic centres will be broken where, in spite of all drawbacks, Islam is, still alive, and the springs of Islamic warmth and eagerness will dry up within us. It will be, then, that the American Islam, European Islam, and the Japanese. Iranian, Indian and Pakistani Islams will emerge, making it impossible to distinguish one from the other. They will be as different from each other as an American is from an Asian, or a Japanese from an Afghan, and Islamic societies will appear whose mental attitudes and natural inclinations and values will be widely apart.

We should take up the challenge and get ready to meet the

threat now when the things have not gone far and the Islamic leaders, are, to some extent, active and effective. The wisdom behind the obligatoriness of the Haj Pilgrimage and the congregation of the Muslims, with all their different social. cultural and linguistic characteristics, at a particular place and at a particular time, is that nothing about Faith remained vague or unclear and stock was taken, at the sametime, of the Muslims of the world and their Islamic lineaments and local innovations and un-Islamic influences they might have accepted owing to the negligence and apathy of the Ulema or as a result of living together, for a considerable length of time. with other peoples and communities could be ascertained and plans evolved for their eradication. As Shah Waliullah has admirably put it, "Had the Haj not been there, the Islamic faith and the Muslims of the East and the West would have been the victims of change and alteration, like the other religions, and it would not have been discovered for ages".

So, brothers, beware of the emergence of a local or territorial Islam and the establishment of Islamic societies that are devoid of the spirit of Islam and built upon foundations that are not genuinely Islamic.

Believe me, it is not a figment of my imagination. I attach the highest importance to it, and, I am sure, when you will go home and think over it you will appreciate the gravity and magnitude of the danger I have indicated.

RESPONSIBILITIES OF MUSLIM IMMIGRANTS

This speech was delivered at Toronto on
June 10, 1977.

VI

O My bondmen who believe ! spacious is My earth ;
therefore serve ye Me (and Me alone)

(—XXIX : 56)

The aim of man's existence, in the sight of God, is
submission, i. e., to attain a true awareness of God, and lead
one's life in conformity with His commands, and seek His
countenance by following the path laid down by the sacred
Prophet, and make provision for the Hereafter. This is the real
aim. All the other things are the means to it. You will, of
course, be knowing the significance of ends and means. The
seeking out of the ways of gaining the propinquity of the Lord,
the creation of a suitable climate for it, and the development of
a critical sense which made it easy to observe the God-given
laws and there remained no question of compulsion or of any
other power to obtrude or give a parallel call—all these are the
means. The Quran has alluded to it in these words :

.... Until there is no more tumult or oppression, and
there prevail justice and faith in Allah.

(—II : 193)

What it denotes is that the state is reached in which Truth
is triumphant and no battles are waged for the souls of men and
they do not have to undergo the ordeal of deciding which way to
turn : only God is obeyed and divine honours are paid to Him
alone. *There prevail justice and faith in Allah.* For it is preaching,
and the sanctioning of what is right and forbidding of what is

wrong. and, if need be, even Jehad. For it is Islam to be made stronger and brought into power and authority so that even for the faint-hearted people it might not become so hard to follow the path indicated by Allah that they gave way to despair and decided that it was beyond their endurance.

So, the end and object of all these things is the worship of Allah. *I created the jinn and humankind only that they might worship Me.* (LI : 56). Let us be clear in our minds for I have noticed a good deal of confusion concerning it in Europe and America. They fail to distinguish between the ends and means. The aim, simply, is to earn the good pleasure of the Lord. Our end and intention ought to be to spend in His way the life and capabilities He has granted us so that the object of life is fulfilled, God is pleased with us on the Day of Resurrection and favours us with His propinquity and we attain the highest place in Paradise. This is the real aim. If it is being realised anywhere then blessed is the place, and if it is not being realised even in one's native land, it should be left for good, Home, parents, wives, children, kinsmen, property, trade—everything must fade into insignificance before duty to God. No worldly attachments should be allowed to stand in its way.

Say : If your fathers, and your sons, and your brethren and your wives, and your tribe, and the wealth ye have acquired, and merchandise for which ye fear that there will be no sale, and dwellings ye desire are dearer to you than Allah and His Messenger and striving in his way : then wait till Allah bringeth His command to pass. Allah guideth not wrong-doing folk.

(—IX : 24)

The charm and attractiveness of Mecca is proverbial. We learn from the Quran that when Hazrat Ibrahim (Abraham) had settled his helpless wife and infant child in that uncultivable valley, he made the prayer : *So incline some hearts of men that they may yearn towards them.* (XIV: 37). The prayer was granted in all respects. Overpowering, really, is the beauty and loveliness of the city of Mecca where there is the Home of Ka'aba, the

Well of Zam Zam, the hills of Safa and Marwa, and, then, close to it are Mina and Arafat. But when the holy Prophet felt that it was becoming extremely difficult for the Muslims to worship God in that wonderful town, he told them to migrate to Abyssinia. He did so in order that they lead their lives in confirmity with the Faith. The Prophet observed: "You cannot worship God here; you cannot offer Namaz; you are forced to bow your heads before the idols; God is treated with insolence in your presence: so, migrate to Abyssinia". Twice did the Muslims move out to Abyssinia. Finally, the Prophet himself was commanded to leave Mecca and go to Medina. If a city like Mecca could be abandoned for the sake of God, in order that He was worshipped in freedom, what to speak to the other towns whether they be New York, London, Toronto, Chicago, Delhi, Lucknow, Kufa, Basra. Cordoba, Granada, Cairo or Damascus. Only that place is beautiful and worth living in where the commands of the Lord can be observed, and where it may not be possible, even if it is one's native land or any other country, it should be left for good.

Brothers!

I travelled to the United States and saw a number of its cities. Now I am here in Canada. On the one hand, it has made me happy to see Muslims belonging to different countries in North America, and, on the other, I wonder if you can lead a fully Islamic life here. Will it be possible for your descendants to remain true to Islam? Will the Islamic spirit abide in you undiminished? It is a serious matter. Do not take offence? Many of you have come here for economic reasons. A brother told me plainly, · We have come here to earn our livelihood." It is not sinful. There is no harm in going to a place where a purely materialistic way of life prevails and heedlessness towards the Futurity is rampant, but the decision to settle down there permanently requires careful consideration. If you are confident that you can live here in confirmity with the will of the Lord, and you are being useful to Islam, and are safeguarding your own faith as well as caring for the faith of others, and are, also, engaged in economic activities according to your needs then it is alright, and I will go on to say that your stay is propitious. God may take from you the task of spreading the guidance in this land, and, one day, it might adopt Islam. It is not inconceivable. When the Muslim traders arrived in the Far East, whole countries were converted to Islam and the Muslims are in a majority in Malaysia and Indonesia and in so many islands of the Indian Ocean even today. If you will care to enquire, you wil know that Islam spread mainly through the efforts of the Arab traders or the Sufi-saints. In my own sub-continent, vast areas like Sind, Kashmir and Bangla Desh are indebted to the Sufi-saints for their conversion to Islam.

Your stay here is not only justified, but also a Jehad if you have made sure of the preservation of Islam for yourselves and your future generations and are carrying out the duty of the preaching and propagation of Faith and presenting an image of the Islamic way of life which is attractive to others. But in case it is otherwise and your aim is simply to make money then it falls much short of the Islamic ideal. It is not worthy of a Muslim to undertake such a long voyage only for economic gain.

The Lord is the Giver of sustenance, and this Attribute of His is not bound down by geographical limitations. I am speaking to you in a practical vein. All this is related wholly to action and practice. You can hear the intellectual subtleties at some other time and from some other theologist. I am only telling you frankly in the light of what I have seen here.

I unequivocally declare that if your life and your stay here are beneficial to Islam and you are paving the way for it, your migration to this land is not only justifiable, but also an act of worship. On the contrary, if your Faith and the religious life of your children are not assured, I shudder at the thought in what state death might come, and, then, would we tell God that we had come here only to earn livelihood. This is neither the Islamic character nor does it befit a Muslim. Nevertheless, if you have taken due care that your Faith remains unblemished, and you are associated with some religious endeavour, and have built up an Islamic environment or founded a circle in which religious activities are promoted and the Lord is remembered and attention is paid to the life of the Hereafter, and you have, also, arranged for the religious instruction of your children then you have my sincere good wishes. This last thing is very important for when, on the Day of Judgement, the children will be asked in what a miserable state they had come that they knew neither the name of God nor of His Apostle, they will reply : *Our Lord ; We obeyed our chiefs and our great ones and they misled us as to the (right) path.*   (—XXXIII : 67).

The Quran says :

O ye who believe ; Ward off from yourselves and your families a Fire whereof the fuel is men and stones.

(—LXVI : 6).

Your children will, of course, be going to school. But, also, set aside for them a couple of hours in which they can receive religious instruction and learn about Monotheism and Apostle-ship, without which no one can be a Muslim, and it is impressed upon them, that it is sinful to die on another Way than Islam : *Die not save as men who have surrendered (unto Him).*

(—II : 132)

Forgive my plain-speaking, but these are some practical things you must give heed to after taking up residence in this country. If you devote a little of your time to the theological education of your progeny and the generation of an Islamic atmosphere then live here by all means. Maybe. God has sent you to this land for it.

I regard the stay of only those Muslims here as justified who have taken adequate steps for the protection of their Faith and made the preaching of the Word of God among the non-Muslims the aim of their life. Or else. even this much is not certain that a Muslim who dies here will be buried according to the Islamic rites.

A relation of mine called, Molvi Mudassir, who is settled in Boston, related to me that as a Haji died. He was told on the phone to participate in the last rites. On reaching there, he found that the dead body of the Haji, dressed in a Western suit, complete with the neck-tie, and wearing a gold ring had been placed in a wooden chest, and Christian men and women were coming in, kissing the body and placing wreaths on the coffin. May God bless Molvi Mudassir with a long life—education in the Arabic Madrassas, after all, bears fruit—, he took the Haji's son aside and told him that he was going back, "Why"? asked the Haji's son, upon which he said, "Will you do what I tell or not"? The Haji's son replied, "I had requested your presence and will act on your advice". "Then", said Molvi Mudassir, "first of all, take off the suit and tell these people to go away from here. I will bathe the dead body and cover it with a shroud as prescribed by the Shariat. And, also, remove the ring", "Do not remove the ring", interjected the Haji's son. "Otherwise, my mother will die of shock" "I shall take off the ring," replied Molvi Mudassir. "If you fear that your mother will die of heart failure, don't tell her now". After much persuasion, the Haji's son agreed and the ring was removed.

A youngman educated in our Madrassas happened to be present at that time, otherwise God alone knows how many Muslims are buried here in that way.

Another similar incident that has come into my knowledge is concerning an Egyptian scholar who was also the author of a book on Islam in English. He had an American wife. When he died, he was buried in a Christian cemetery as the Muslim graveyard was at a distance.

Happenings like these are so horrible that even if a Muslim saw them in a dream, he would scream, "Oh God! Have mercy on me". Fie upon us that they became common and we remained unmoved.

So, brothers, care for yourselves and for your children, and see to it that they remained Muslims. Otherwise your immigration makes no sense to me. You are in danger and so is your country. Had the brain drain not continued unchecked and the youngmen who are coming to settle down here from India and

Pakistan stayed back, they would have been a source of strength to their communities, subordinates and parents. The number of Arabs in America is increasing day by day. They could have proved a great asset to their native lands if they had decided not to migrate. Coming here merely for larger salaries and better living conditions is beyond my comprehension. It is a question upon which serious thought must be bestowed.

GOODWILL AND AFFECTION AMONG THOSE WHO STRIVE FOR FAITH CANNOT BE PRODUCED BY ARTIFICIAL MEANS

This speech was delivered at the 15th Convention of Muslim Students Association of the United States and Canada. The audience included educationists, writers, historians and economists.

VII

Gentleman !

The subject for today's discussion is 'Mutual contacts and relations among those who work for the propagation and preservation of Islam.' I will try to shed some light on it, but it, will, perhaps, not be necessary for me to stick to its literal meaning. My attempt will be to indicate the real origin of these bonds and sentiments.

I believe that love and fellow-feeling cannot be generated among Tabligh[1] workers through external means. No substance has yet been discovered which can join the hearts. The spring-head of love is found within the heart of man. It cannot be brought in from outside. Nothing in the world can unite the hearts which do not feel drawn towards each other or are not governed by a common feeling or reality. It is not like joining stones in a buliding or sticking pieces of paper together. Says the Quran :

> If thou hadst spent all that is in the earth thou couldst not have attuned their hearts (i. e., the hearts of the Believers).

(—VIII :63)

It shows that unity could not have been produced among the Believers, at any cost and by any means, had Allah not joined their hearts.

---

1. Meaning preaching and propagation of Islam.

As you are aware, when the Muslims migrated from Mecca to Medina there was nothing in common between the Mohajirs[1] and the Ansars[2] except the Arabic language. Even racially they were different from one another. The Mohajirs belonged to the Arabian tribes of Bani Adnan while the Ansars to the Yemenite tribles of Bani Qahtan. Yet an unexampled accord and feeling of oneness was created between them. Concerning it, the Quran says :

And remember Allah's favour unto you : how ye were enemies and He made friendship between your hearts so that ye became as brothers by His grace.

(—III : 103)

It was the miracle of this brotherly feeling that when the Mohajirs reached Medina, the Ansars settled them not only in their homes, but, also, in their hearts. The Ansar said to the Mohajir : "This is my house : half of it is mine and half of it is yours. Take whichever part you like". In the same way, the Ansars willingly agreed to give half of their agricultural lands and other property to the Mohajirs, so much so that some of them said that they had two wives, one of whom they were ready to divorce so that his Mohajir brother could marry her. And what did the Mohajirs do ? They acted with dignity. Instead of seizing greedily what the Ansars offered, they said : "Brothers, may God grant you an increase in your riches. Show us the way to the market and we will try our luck there."

Such warmth and earnestness, obviously, cannot be produced by artificial means. As you are aware, to bring about unity in their ranks has always been a major problem with all human associations.

I will give a few examples to illustrate the point, and, then, try to explain what is the real springhead of oneness and

---

1. Literally, the 'emigrants'. Here it shows the Muslims of Mecca who had migrated to Medina and taken up residence there.
2. Literally, it means the 'helpers'. In Islamic terminology it applies to the inhabitants of Medina who first embraced the Islamic faith and extended warm support and hospitality to the emigrants from Mecca.

solidarity.   These examples have been taken from the biography of the sacred Prophet.

Abu Aziz bin Omair was one of the Pagans of Mecca who had been taken prisoner in the Battle of Badr.   His real brother, Mus'ab bin Omair, was the standard-bearer of the Islamic forces. He had migrated to Medina earlier.   When the hands of Abu Aziz bin Omair were being tied behind his back, Mus'ab bin Omair told the man who was doing it to tie hard and true as he was a rich man and would pay a good ransom.   Upon it, Abu Aziz bin Omair said, "Brother, I had expected that you would put in a kind word on my behalf and tell him to tie my hands gently as I was your own brother, but you are telling him to bind firmly so that a large sum of money could be realised from me for my liberation." Mus'ab bin Omair's reply will always be remembered in the annals of moral and spiritual revolutions. He observed, "You are not my brother, but he who is tying your hands".

Unity of faith and loftiness of purpose had brought about such a transformation in the life of Mus'ab bin Omair that he bluntly told his brother that "now the man who is tying your hands is my brother and not you because a new bond has sprung up between us which, though it has nothing to do with blood, is much more precious than the ties of kinship and lineage."

In the same manner, it is related by a Companion, Abu Jahm bin Huzaifa, that "once, during the Battle of Yarmuk, I went into the battle-field in search of my cousin. I knew that those who are wounded in a battle are tormented by thirst, and, so, I was carrying a small water-bag with me with the thought that he might be in his dying moments and I will pour some water in his mouth and wash his face. When I reached my cousin, I found that he was in the pangs of death, and his lips were parched. I offered him a cup of water, but, in the meantime, a groan was heard and my cousin said, 'This brother of mine is in greater need of water. Give the cup to him and leave me to fate'. So, I went to him and as I was offering him the drink, the groan of another man was heard upon which he requested me to give the water to him. It went on like that and when I carried the cup to one wounded person, he pointed out towards another till I returned to my cousin and saw that he had breathed his last. I, thereupon, went to the second man, and, then, to the third man, and, so on, only to find that they, too, were dead. My cup remained untouched, and those deep-hearted bondmen went to meet their Maker without taking a sip from it."

The third incident I would like to refer is even more amazing. When the Battle of Yarmuk was being fought, right in the thick of it, Caliph Omar decided to relieve General Khalid bin Valeed of the command of the Islamic forces and appoint Abu Obaida in his place. General Khalid had become a legendary figure around whom the myth of invincibility had grown on account of his glorious exploits in war, and it was, perhaps, why Caliph Omar wanted to replace him. He did not want the impression to gain strength that Khalid and victory went together, and instead of God, people began to rely upon him for overcoming the enemy. When the order of the dismissal of Khalid was received, preparation were being made for mounting a decisive attack and Caliph Omar had ordered that the headgear of General Khalid should be taken off and wound around his neck so that people knew that he had been dismissed. The General showed not a trace of sorrow or anger when the order was communicated to him. With unbelievable calmness he said: "I believe and I submit. There will be no change in my conduct. If I was fighting for God, I shall still fight, and if I was fighting for Omar, I have every right to withdraw for he has expressed lack of faith in me and deprived me of a such an honour." He continued to fight with his usual skill and bravery. The dismissal made no difference to his determination and enthusiasm while in the so-called advanced societies of the present times we see that if a person is relieved of his office he is affected with loathing and becomes sulky and glum.

Unity of faith, unity of purpose and unity of love can bring forth marvellous results, provided that the faith, cause of love is all-pervading.   Mere association or agreement is not enough. It is a great folly to think that agreement with an aim is sufficient.   One should be in love with it.   The incidents I have just described take place when the candle-moth relationship is established between a cause and those who strive for it.

I have mentioned here four incidents belonging to the eras of the sacred Prophet and the holy Companions which served to illustrate what a wounderful unity and spirit of sacrifice the oneness of faith and devotion to the cause had produced among the followers of Islam. But you can say that is was the golden age of Islam when the hearts had been purged of sin and immorality. It is stated in the Quran :

> But Allah hath endeared the faith to you and hath beautified it in your hearts, and hath made disbelief and lewdness and rebellion hateful unto you.

(—XLIX : 7)

"Are instances of such a refulgent class and quality, also, found after that period of blessedness and glory had ended ?", you may ask. These, you, may add, will be of greater value to you since you belong to the times that are far removed from the era of Apostleship and encourage you to seek inspiration from them in this, the 20th Century.

I submit that history will repeat itself and astonishing events like these will recur if the hold of faith is firm, commitment to the cause is complete, and a reformer or benefactor is found who dyes everyone in the same hue.

At present, I will relate to you only two incidents that took place in course of the struggle launched by Syed Ahmad Shaheed (martyred May 6, 1831) for the revival of Islam. Not much time has passed since then, and, what is more, these appertain to the days when the British had dug their feet in India and Muslim society had come considerably under the influence of the Western Civilization.

Molvi Abdul Wahab of Lucknow was incharge of the distribution of foodgrains at Panjtar, the headquarters of

Syed Saheb's army of Mujahids.[1] His practice was that he recited the Quran while distributing the flour etc., and sometimes, gave the quota of twenty or twenty-five persons to one man without counting, but everyone received his portion and no one got more or less than his allotted share.

One day, as he was distributing the flour, Mir Imam Ali Azimabadi came for his daily allowance. He was a very powerfully-built man. The flour was being dealt out turn by turn to the Mujahids, and the Mir was in a hurry. He wanted to be served before those who had come earlier. Molvi Abdul Wahab told him to await his turn, but he would not listen and pushed Molvi Saheb so hard that he fell down.

Some Qandharis,[2] also, were sitting there, waiting for their turn. They were annoyed at the behaviour of Mir Imam Ali and rushed at him. But Molvi Abdul Wahab checked them, saying, "He is my brother. If he pushed, he pushed me. What have you to do with it ?" The incident was reported to Syed Saheb and when Molvi Abdul Wahab went to see him in the evening, he enquired from him about what Mir Imam Ali had done. "As far as I am concerned," replied the Molvi, "he did nothing. He is a very good man. He had come for his allowance of flour but it was not his turn, and he did not like to wait. In the meantime, he collided against me. That was all." When Mir Imam Ali came to know of what Molvi Abdul Wahab had said about him, he felt deeply ashamed and apologised to the Molvi and embraced him in Syed Saheb's presence.

A more inspiring incident which reminds one of the earliest decades of Islam is that of Lahori who, also, was a member of the glorious band of Mujahids who had collected around Syed Ahmad Shaheed.

It is related in *Seerat-i-Syed Ahmad Shaheed* that once Lahori who was a very simple-minded man, and, jointly with

---

1. Meaning warriors in the defence of Islam.
2. Meaning the inhabitants of Qandhar in Afghanistan.

Sheikh Inayatullah, looked after the preparation of fodder for the horses, got angry with the Sheikh over something. Upon it, Sheikh Inayatullah, who was very close to Syed Saheb, got unnecessarily agitated, and in the altercation that followed, he delivered such a blow on Lahori's head that he dropped on the ground and began to moan. When Syed Saheb heard about it, he reproved Sheikh Inayatullah severely and said, you would be thinking that you were an old colleague of mine and slept near my cot. but you did not remember that we had come here for the sake of God and yet did such shameful things. You thought that Lahori was the Sais[1] of Qazi Madni and he was a very poor and ugly-looking person, and you hit him for that reason. You have done a great wrong. With me you and Lahori are alike. No one has a superiority over the other. We all have come here to serve the cause of God."

After it, Syed Saheb told Hafiz Sabir Thanvi and Sharfuddin Bengali to take Lahori and Inayatullah to the Qazi and tell him to decide according to the Shariat and show no leniency.

On the next day, in the forenoon, Hafiz Sabir and Sharfuddin produced Lahori and Inayatullah before the Qazi who made them sit before him, and, turning first to Inayatullah, rebuked him sternly, and said that he had done a very wrong thing for which he deserved to be punished. Then, addressing Lahori, the Qazi remarked, "Brother, you are a very good and harmless person. You all have left your homes in Hindustan and come to this distant place solely for waging war in the way of God so that He may be pleased with you and reward you in the Hereafter. As for this world, it is a nine days' wonder. So, the thing is that Inayatullah is your brother and he has committed this offence and assaulted you out of misforturne. If you forgive him, it will be very good and God will recompense you in the Hereafter for it, and if you take the revenge, you will be quits but you will not get the reward that is promised

---

1. Meaning a man-servant in charge of horses.

on forgiving. To forgive is the command of God and the Apostle, and so is to take revenge. But there is a reward on forgiving and satisfaction of self in taking the revenge".

On hearing it, Lahori said, "Qazi Saheb! I will get the reward if I forgive Inayatullah, and if I avenge myself, we will be quits; but will there be any sin in it?" "There will be no sin," replied the Qazi. "Both are the commands of God and the Apostle. Choose whichever you like. "Then I demand my right," said Lahori. After a pause, the Qazi observed, "Brother Lahori, your right is that you hit Inayatullah at the same place where he had hit you." He made Inayatullah stand before Lahori and told the latter to take his revenge. "My right is that I strike him twice at that very place. Is it not?" asked Lahori. "Of course," the Qazi replied.

Those who were witnessing the trial were filled with consternation; they felt sure that Lahori would not let Inayatullah go without having his revenge. But Lahori had other ideas. He said, "Well, brothers, you are a witness to the fact that the Qazi has upheld my claim. I can take the revenge. But I forego it for the good pleasure of the Lord." He, then, embraced Inayatullah and shook hands with him. With one voice, everyone complimented Lahori and said that he had done what only a truly devout and godly man could do.

No one can attain this moral stature without a genuine love for God and the Apostle, and the love for God and the Apostle cannot be produced simply by study and reflection or listening to the speeches. I am appreciative of the papers that have been read and the speeches that have delivered here, but on careful thought, you will agree that this is not the way to the generation of love. A deep study of the life, sayings and doings of the Prophet is essential for the promotion of the sentiments of deep devotion and self-abnegation, and it should not be a formal one, but capable of going down deep into one's moral and spiritual nature.

The honour you have done me and the affection and trust you have shown and the long journey I have undertaken to be with you demand that I presented the sum and substance of my knowledge and experience before you which is that there is nothing more precious, dynamic and inspiring in the vast treasure-house of Islam than the Quran and the biography of the Prophet. The Book of God, the holy Quran, is something we can, honestly, be proud of. It is the greatest fountain-head of strength and vitality by means of which we can subjugate the hearts, subdue the propensities of the self and overcome the desires of the flesh. It can transform our lives and lift us from the lowness of the earth to the height of the skies. With its help we can confront the Devil and frustrate his designs. Springs of powers and energy that gushed forth from it in the earliest decades have not dried up. Next, is the biography of the that Prophet. I would appeal you must fervently develop the strongest attachment, firstly, for the Quran, and, then, for the biography of the Prophet. The biography of the sacred Prophet can still bring about a revolution in the lives of men and give rise to a new Ummat.[1]

Self-indulgence, self-worship and self-seeking have always been the bane of the Muslims. We have never been harmed or humbled by our enemies. It is on account of our own internal strifes and dissensions that we have suffered defeats and lost empires.

Take the case of Spain. The largest single factor leading to the ejection of Islam from that land were our internecine quarrels. I refuse to believe that it was the might of Christianity alone that forced Islam and Muslims out of Spain. No mean part was played by the mutual rivalries of the Northen Arabs, the Yemenite Arabs and the Hejazis that had been rife for a long time. It were the suicidal wars among the Yemenites, the Hejazis, the Rabi'a and the Muzir that culminated in the banishment of Islam, and, Spain, in the words of Iqbal, was deprived of the Azan.[2]

1. Meaning community.
2. Muslim call to prayers, generally proclaimed from the minarets or towers of a mosque.

Thy land is like the heavens in the sight of the stars,
For ages, alas, thy atmosphere has remained bereft of
Azan.

The same story has been repeated in most of the Islamic countries. In India, too, the downfall of the Mughal Empire was brought about, mainly, by domestic feuds and factions and intrigues and uprisings.

The malady of self-seeking and earthly-mindedness cannot be overcome only by sermons and seminars. To subdue anything you have to use a more powerful agent. If we have to put down fire, we pour water on it, and for heating up iron, we ignite the fire. Selfishness and self-worship cannot be wished away, and unity and brotherly love are not engendered by public discourses and pious declarations.

When personal, tribal or factional interests are given preference over the aims and interests of Islam, it will lead to the same disastrous results that have overtaken the Indian Muslims.

When I was in Europe, I said, again and again, to my Muslim brothers who had settled there :

"You are faced with a tremendous trail. On the day of Final Judegement, the Lord will call you to account and the holy Prophet will enquire. We had given you a very large field in which you could raise the banner of Islamic renaissance and give the call of Faith and subdue the conquerors of the world, but you started rushing at each-other's throats and got involved in mutual quarrels and destructive struggles for power. Now, what answer will you give ?"

Gentlemen! The springhead of love is in the heart. Mutual affection, sympathy and fellow-felling cannot be produced by external means and without the love of God, and the love of God is generated by offering Namaz, shedding tears, making earnest entreaties to Him, and praying in the silent hours of the night for elevation in the ranks of believing brethren :

"Our Lord! Forgive us and our brethren who were before us in the faith and place not in our hearts any rancour towards those who believe. Our Lord! Thou art

Full of Pity, Merciful.

(—LIX : 10)

The interest of Islam must prevail over all other interests.

People have forgiven their bitterest enemies. I will tell you of an incident. Once a person suspected a very godly man to have stolen his purse, and without any proof or enquiry, started beating him like any thing. Other people intervened and scolded him for his meanness. The man realised his mistake and apologised to the holy man. Upon it. the holy man said, "Brother, there is no question of an apology. When you were beating me, I was beseeching the Lord that 'Oh God ! If Thou hast decided that I entered Paradise then I will not set my foot in it until Thou alloweth this man, also, who is beating me, to enter with me. I was making this prayer. What to speak of having a grievance against you ?"

We should keep these life-patterns before us. We will find such instances in the biography of the sacred Prophet and the life-accounts of the holy Companions. Study the biography of the Prophet thoroughly and well. Go Back from here with the resolve that you will make the biography of the Prophet your constant companion and seek guidance from it. Also, read as much as possible. about the life and character of the blessed Companions. Correct your Namaz. We are the bondmen of the Lord. If we do not set right our bond with God, and our hearts are not imbued with love for Him, we can never feel sincerely for His bondmen, nor be truly high-minded and self-sacrificing for the mainspring of all these qualities and emotions, in Islam, is the love of God and the Prophet.

TO THE MUSLIM LADIES

This speech was delivered at the seminar of Muslim Women at Chicago on June 19, 1977.

VIII

Brothers and Sisters !

I am deeply indebted to you for inviting me to this meeting and giving me an opportunity to express my views on a question which is fundamentally related to existence, both social and individual.

At the outset. I will recite a verse of the Quran, and, then, try to explain the Islamic viewpoint on social relations, and indicate how realistic it is in its approach to community life.

The verse is from *Sura-i-Nissa* (the Chapter of Women). Its very title should be enough to show what place Islam gives to womankind.

It reads :

> O Mankind ! Be careful of your duty to your Lord Who created you from a single soul (i. e., Adam) and from it created its mate and from them twain hath spread abroad a multiude of men and women. Be careful of your duty towards Allah through Whom you demand your mutual (rights), and towards the wombs (that bare you).
>
> Lo ! Allah hath been a Watcher over you.

(—IV : 1)

I believe this verse fully explains the Islamic standpoint on the status of women and the mutual rights and duties of the two sexes. First of all, God makes it clear that both men and women have been created in the same manner and their destinies are inter-related, as if they are the two parts of a single body. The little divergence in their physical structures is for no other reason than that they performed the journey of life comfortably.

Both the male and female groups have been created from a single soul, and, then, that single soul has been divided into two parts, but there is no contradiction or hostility between them. In life's journey, man has been provided with a partner from his own species and who is a part of his body. After it, the human race took its rise from them. God blessed their union, love and companionship with great abundance so that those who were, originally, two multiplied into millions till no one can tell how many men have been born into the world. It is known only to God. He has alluded to their abundance by using the word 'multitude'.

The Lord, then says : Fear Allah in Whose Name you lay your claim on one another. The revolutionary idea that in the economy of human affairs, no one is sufficient into himself was, for the first time, propounded by the Quran. All men are dependent on one another. Everyone is, at once, the beggar and the giver. The division is not such that the beggars are one side and the givers on the other. The beggar is, also, the giver, and vice versa. Everyone is tied to the chain of rights and duties. In the network of civilised life everybody stands in need of others.

Without a woman, no man can accomplish his natural journey in a pleasant and comfortable manner, and, in the same way, no virtuous woman can lead a happy and contented life without a life-partner. The Lord Creator has made them dependent on each other in such a way that without one, the life of the other must remain incomplete.

Again, it is proclaimed that it is Allah in whose Name you demand your rights of one another. The Islamic society is founded upon belief in God, in His Power, Majesty and Oneness. The partnership between a Muslim man and a Muslim woman becomes legitimate when the Name of Allah is brought in between them. It is the Name of Allah that makes the strangers, the kindred, and the distant ones, the near ones.

The bond between man and wife is a bond of faith and love, and in its depth, intimacy and naturalness; it is absolutely unique. All this is the miracle of the Name of Allah. A new world is born with the coming in of His Name. A Muslim man and a Muslim woman cannot mix freely with one another; sometimes, they cannot even travel together. They are *Na Mahram*[1] to each other. But a sacred tie is forged as soon as the Name of Allah comes to dwell between them.

The Quran, in its inimitable style, has represented the basic reality of human society, interdependence of its members, their co-relation and mutuality, in the few. simple words of *through Whom ye demand your mutual rights.*

It, then, proceeds to urge upon us to be careful of our duty to Allah in whose Name we make the unlawful, lawful, and bring about a revolution in our lives. The Quran has used another matchless expression, also, to describe the profound relationship between husband and wife. It says: *They are raiment for you and ye are raiment for them.* (II : 187). It was Quran alone that could use the word *raiment* in that context. Clothing is essential for hiding nakedness and for adornment of life. It conveys everything that can be said concerning the relationship of love, faith and trust between husband and wife. Just as without clothing a man looks more like an animal than a civilised being, in the same way, without a married life, must be considered less than civilised.

In Islam matrimony is not regarded a necessity but given the status of worship which brings a man closer to God. Or, in other words, the concept of marriage in it is not that of a biological or social necessity without which the enjoyment of life is not complete, but it has been given religious significance and elevated to the position of worship. The sacred Prophet furnished the greatest example of it in his own life. He said,

1. A stranger. One who is not permitted to enter women's apartment.

"The best among you is he who is good to his family, and, among you, I am the best for my family." If you study the life of the Prophet. you will be struck by instances of showing respect to the fair sex and paying regard to its sentiments which are not to be found in the lives of the greatest champions of the rights of women or of holy men and law-givers of the highest order. and even in the lives of the other Apostles. The pains the holy Prophet took to please his wives and make them happy, his participation in their legitimate recreational activities and doing of justice to them were of surpassing charm and nobleness.

With children, also, he was so kind and affectionate that he would even cut short Namaz, which was so dear to his heart, if he heard a child crying. It was the height of benevolence and sacrifice. Nothing could be more precious to the holy Prophet than Namaz. Yet, he would say, "Sometimes. I like to prolong the prayer-service. but, then, I hear a child crying and shorten the service, thinking that its mother would be restless."

These are the examples we have before us. The Lord exhorts us to protect the dignity of the Name we have brought in. It should not be that we put it only to our advantage. This commandment is for both, men and women. You are, now, living in the American society. We have not only to introduce the tenets of Islam to the American people, but, also, to present before them living models of its family-system. The Western Civilisation is rapidly on decline. There can be no two opinions about it. One of the foremost reasons of it is the disintegration of the family. Love and trust which are the cornerstone of a married life are yielding place to selfishness and sensuality. Modern philosophers are worried and studies are being undertaken for the preservation of the sanctity of the family. There ought to be love and sympathy on both the sides for in it, alone, lies true happiness. Even poverty and starvation are tolerated with equanimity where there is love and willingness to enter into and share the feelings of one another. There are, even now, many families in the East which do not have enough to eat and yet live happily because their is mutual love. Here, in the West there is everything—wealth, scientific innovation, and educational advancement—,but the hearts are devoid of peace and contentment.   They have not been able to turn their homes into a paradise.   As Iqbal has said :

>He sought the orbits of the stars, yet could not
>Travel his own thought's world.

The modern man is equipped with power, but lacking in vision.   The conqueror of the solar radiation could not brighten his own destiny, and the seeker of the orbits of the stars—and, if Iqbal were alive today, he would have said, the traveller to the moon—could not explore the world of his own ideas and make his home a place of bliss.   He who had set out to turn the world into a paradise has ended up by making his own home a hell.   Many Western homes are unblest with peace and happiness.   That is why, they seek diversion in clubs and other out-door activities.

You will be more aware of this painful aspect of American life as you have been living here for as many as ten or twenty years.   It will be futile for me to dwell upon it at length.   The Quranic verse I have quoted expounds the fundamental truth of Islamic social design that human society is based upon inter-dependence and respect for each others's rights.   Everyone has his needs.   But to realise it as a basic truth of human existence and to feel grateful to the person through whom the need is fulfilled is an attitude of mind.   Islam' seeks to promote and strengthen that outlook.   It wants everyone to consider himself dependent on others and entertain respect for all members of the society.   No problems of adjustment will, then, arise.

May Allah guide you to the Straight Path and you are able to present the pattern of Islamic life and social conduct that may be appealing to the Western people who have grown weary of life and encourage them to think over and examine closely the social commandments of Islam !

You will, thus, be rendering valuable service not only to this country, but also to Islam.   It is difficult to think of a more positive and effective step towards the preaching and propaga-tion of Faith in the existing circumstances.

PROTECTION OF FAITH MUST TAKE PRECEDENCE OVER EVERYTHING : ACKNOWLEDGE THE SERVICES OF PIOUS PRECURSORS AND ENTERTAIN RESPECT FOR THEM

This speech was delivered at the Muslim Community Centre of Chicago on June 20, 1977. As there was a very representative gathering and it was going to be the last speech of the tour, the Maulana thought it fit to restate briefly what he had seen and felt during his stay in that part of the world, and, also, offer some suggestions.

IX

Brothers, Sisters and Friends !

I have been journeying through the United States and Canada for the last there weeks. During it, I have made dozens of speeches in Urdu and Arabic. But a speech is, after all, a formal public discourse in which there is the force of eloquence as well as repetition of ideas. Today, I will talk to you informally, like a family-member. I will give some personal impressions, and offer a few suggestions, and shall feel obliged if you will think over them seriously.

After meeting different people and representatives of different organisations, I have arrived at certain conclusions. There are, as it were, the gains of the present visit for which I am deeply grateful to M.S.A. and other well-wishers. I pray to God and beg you, also, to join me in the prayer that at todays meeting, I may say only what is going to be useful and beneficial to you in the long run, and this journey of mine does not turn out to be an exercise in futility, for I am often assailed by the doubt whether I have proved really worthy of all the trouble. It has been a long and expensive affair and friends have spared no pains to make it possible   Now, will I not be called to account by God for it ? May be, I have committed mistakes during the trip and failed to live upto expectations. What I am going to say, today, may serve as an atonement for my failings. There is no dearth of speeches, and it has, also, become customary to put questions to the speaker at the end of a speech. In the midst of it all, however, the real thing is forgotten. Often it so happens that during a speech the listeners begin to formulate questions in their minds. I hope you will not indulge in the exercise until I have finished.

First of all, I will ask you earnestly to protect the wealth of Islam you possess. Do not lose it at any cost. If you realised how short was the life of world and how long the life of futurity and through what stages were you going to pass in the Hereafter, your hair would stand on end. Who will be more unfortunate than ourselves if we did everything here in America but allowed the provision of the fear of God and solicitiude for the Hereafter to go to waste. I swear by God that it would have been much better to starve than to invite the risk and imperil the religious future of our children. We will be the greatest losers if we gained everything, but lost the wealth of Faith.

The Apostle of God said, "One of the three qualities essential for tasting the sweetness of faith is that the idea of going back to Apostasy after a man has embraced Islam is as dreadful to him as being thrown into fire."

Let us not, by our conduct, be the verifiers of the truth of these verses of the Quran

> Shall We tell you of those who lose most in respect of their deeds? Those whose efforts have been wasted in this life, while they thought they were acquiring good by their works?

(—XVIII : 103-104)

The poor souls belived that they were acquiring good by their works ! This is the moral of these verses. What I fear is that it might be applying to us. Many people know that they are doing wrong when they are guilty of a reprehensible or immoral act. But a peculiarity of the modern civilisation is that it never occurs to a man that he can err. He is so smug and self-satisfied. For instance, if one enquires from anyone in India or Pakistan where his brother was and what he was doing, he will reply with a twinkle in his eye, *"Masha Allah,* He is in America and earning so many thousand dollars." This is what is being said back home. Here, on our part. we say, "How well have we done ? What would we be earning had we stayed in Hyderabad, Uttar Pradesh, Bihar, Lahore or Karachi? Here we are getting more than what a Governor or Minister in India or Pakistan gets ?"

Be on your guard against this frame of mind and prefer the security and preservation of Faith to every kind of worldly success so that you do not depart from this world save as truthful Muslims. I say that a man who lives in America and takes the Faith unimpaired with him to the next world will, perhaps, merit a greater reward than him who dies in Arabia because he protects the lamp of his faith against all sorts of storms and tempests. It is related that the Apostle of God said:

> "Some of my brothers will be steadfast in Faith and observe their duty to God." "Are we not your brothers '? asked the Companions. "You are my Companions," replied the Prophet, "but my brothers are those who have not seen me. They will be born much later and their faith will be on the unseen, i. e., they will embrace Islam without seeing me."

Believe me, you can attain the highest grade of spiritual excellence in America and the good work you do here will be infinitely more pleasing to the Lord because the mother feels more strongly for her child when it is far off from her and prays more earnestly for its safety. You are the children of Islam who are placed far away from its cradle and surrounded by forces of Apostasy and Materialism. You will, therefore, be receiving the special attention of God. Do not despair of His Mercy.

Give precedence to Islam in all circumstances. Poverty with Faith is a million times better than power and wealth that are without it. By the grace of God, you are an intelligent and educated people· Should there be the least danger to Faith, go back to your native land or to any other place where there may the security of Faith, along with your family, even if you have to do it on foot. Whatever the conditions, your endeavour should be to live upto the Divine Commandment : *And die not save as men who have surrendered (unto Him).*   (II : 132).

Next, let all your deeds be intended for seeking the countenance of the Lord and no other consideration, like that of place or position, should prevail. Worldly gain will, *Insha Allah*, come your way according to your ability and application, but take care of your intention so that you may receive the due reward on what you do. As a Tradition of the Prophet reads :

"The actions are judged according to intentions, and to every man is due what he intended. Thus, whosoever migrates for the sake of Allah and His Apostle, his migration is accounted for the sake of Allah and His Apostle; and whosoever migrates for the sake of this world or to wed a woman, it will be accounted only for the purpose for which it is intended."

Look into your intention from time to time, and make it right. The aim and idea behind all your acts should be the propitiation of the Lord and the service of Islam and Muslims. You will, then, *Insah Allah*, earn the reward equal in value to that on Jehad, and, sometimes, even on martyrdom.

Your effort should be to do everything with *Iman* (faith in God) and *Ihtisab* (confident expectation of Divine recompense). A deed carries weight with God only when it is performed with *Iman* and *Ihtisab*. For example, it is stated in a Tradition about the fasts of Ramzan that "whoever keeps the fasts of Ramzan with *Iman* and *Ihtisab*, all his previous sins will be forgiven".

You may well ask how can fasting be observed with *bad-niyati* (badness of intention). Brothers, *bad-niyati* is one thing; *be-niyati* (absence of intention) is another; and, as I often say, the Muslims are more a victim of *be-niyati* than *bad-niyati*. At the time of performing a deed they care not to ask themselves whether they are doing it with the intention of pleasing the Lord or out of habit or custom.

Thirdly, do not be self-complacent. Look inward, into your own heart and mind. Keep your deeds under constant review. Cultivate the habit of self-criticism. Be your own examiner. I will advise you to visit your native countries regularly, every two years or so. Maintain a living contact with the places of your origin. It would be better if you could go to India, Pakistan or the cities of Mecca and Medina and spend some time there in a religious environment and in the company of virtuous and godly men. The wells of religious fervour and God-consciousness would dry up within you if you went on living here without a break. The battery of the heart must be charged from time to time by going to your country and passing a few months in it. I have noticed that there is a marked difference between those who maintain a contact with their native lands and those who do not. People who are out of touch with their home-countries, generally, develop an insensitiveness towards religious feelings, values and ideals.

Even if they offer Namaz and observe fasting, it is in a routine manner. I agree that this, too, is not unavailing, but they grow indifferent to the spiritual content of these acts. They fail to appreciate their solidity and have no idea of the state of the chosen bondmen of the Lord and of the quality of their prayers and the depth and intensity of their feelings.

Religious environment is in the nature of a power-house. By the grace of God, this environment still exists in India and Pakistan and men of high moral and spiritual stature are found in whose company the rust is removed from the hearts. I am saying it from personal experience. The same way have I felt even in Saudi Arabia which I visit frequently. There, also, I have observed that families who have remained in contact with India are in a much better shape than those who have adopted the Arab culture and severed their ties with India. Mecca and

Medina are, of course, the real centres of Islam, but they, too, have started accepting thoughtlessly the influence of the Western Civilisation and the petro-dollars are playing havoc with the social and cultural values of the Arabs. What is more, a sort of complacency is created when people take up residence in those blessed cities. We are the inhabitants of Hejaz, we live under the shadow of the House of Ka'aba—this is how they begin to feel. One the contrary, religious condition of those is, definitely, better who maintain a living contact with India make regular visits to it, do not lose touch with Urdu in which religious books and magazines are published, and make the theologians and spiritual mentors coming from India and Pakistan their guests and learn the laws and principles of the Shariat from them; they go more frequently to Mecca and Medina, perform the Umra[1] more often and bear a greater attachment for the sacred town of Medina.

Fourthly, you live in America, and are, also, interested in the Islamic literature. I have seen that there is a growing demand in the United States and Canada for good religious books in English and Urdu, and theologians, writers and leaders from Islamic countries come here and meetings are arranged in their honour. Now, I want to impress upon you one thing : do not deprecate the pious precursors and think ill of those who have served the cause of Faith in their own spheres. It is a most dangerous trend and a grave folly. Our brothers whose knowledge is derived solely from books are, generally, more prone to it. When they read such articles or books they jump to the conclusion that no one had yet under-taken a thorough study of Islam. In their immature minds they form a tapeline for measuring the service to Faith, and proceed to pronounce judgement on every reformer on the basis of it.

You have no idea of the difficult circumstances in which

---

1. Pilgrimage to Mecca at any time of the year apart from the days of the Haj.

these deep-hearted men had carried out their mission. I can only sympathise with him who, for instance, blames Sheikh Abdul Qadir Jilani for spending all his time in giving sermons and caring nothing for the establishment of an Islamic State, although, in his days, the Abbasid Caliph had suspended the Islamic order.

Gentlemen ! Are you not aware of the magnificient work done by this illustrious man of God ? Africa is still indebted to him for it was through his Order that Islam spread there, and similar has been the case with India, Indonesia and many other countries. God alone knows how many dead hearts were reanimated by him and how many men were delivered from Apostasy and Polytheism to Islam through his efforts. He knew that the Abbasid Caliphs belonged to the family of the sacred Prophet; they were Arabs and Hashmites, and understood the Quran as well as he did. Then, why did they not acquit themselves in a fitting manner as the Caliphs of Islam ? He was convinced that at the root of it lay the excessive fondness for power and wealth. So, he set himself to the task of the moral and spiritual regeneration of the society as a whole. I ask you what is wrong with Pakistan ? Is that country and its rulers not Muslims ? Had it not been created in the name of Islam ? Only the other day a Pakistani friend was telling me that a youngman who was related to him had joined a procession that was being taken out at Lyallpur to protest against the Government. Some-one in the procession raised the slogan, "On what was the founda-tion of Pakistan laid ?" "*On La illaaha, illallaah, Mohammadur rasulullaah,*" replied the youngman. He had hardly finished the sentence that a bullet hit him in the chest and he dropped dead on the ground.[1] Now, tell me, whether the shot was fired by a Muslim or a non-Muslim ? Why is it happening ? Why is a Muslim killing a Muslim ? If a person sincerely believed that the malaise was due primarily to headlong

1. It should be noted that the incident took place in the days of Mr. Zulfikar Ali Bhutto, after the last General Elections.

absorption in worldly aims and pleasures and spent his life fighting against it, what was wrong with it.

Sometimes, it is imagined that if anyone did not work for the establishment of an Islamic State, he simply wasted his time and did nothing, no matter whether he was Sheikh Abdul Qadir Jilani, Mujaddid Alf-Sani or Shah Waliullah. This is owing to an imperfect reading of history. I say without hesitation that if Islam is safe and alive in the world, today, the credit for it does not go to any one section of the Ummat. The theologians, the jurists, the scholars of the Traditions, the religious teachers, the spiritual mentors and the Sufi-saints have all played their part.

Were anyone to assert that Imam Abu Hanifa only taught the rules and proprieties of Namaz and Roza while he should have seized power and established an Islamic State, then, my friends, the Islamic State would have come into being, but who would have been there to teach how Namaz was to be offered ? And of what worth is a Caliphate in which no one knows how to say Namaz ?

Those who, if We give them power in the land, establish worship and pay the poor-due and enjoin what is right and forbid iniquity. And Allah's is the sequel of events.

(—XXII : 41)

The Quran does not say that those whom We will teach how to offer Namaz will establish the Islamic Government, but that power and rule is meant for paving the way for Namaz so that there remained no excuse for neglect.

Says the Lord : *Until persecution is no more, and religion is all for Allah.* (VIII : 39)

Never imagine that those who preceded us were worthless men, none of whom understood Islam or tried to establish the whole of it, in form as well as in spirit. In fact, they all were doing their best to serve the cause of Faith : someone was giving sermons, someone was teaching the Traditions, someone was issuing religious decrees and someone was writing books.

According to his aptitude and circumstances, everyone of them was engaged in the propagation and preservation of Islam and moral and spiritual instruction of Muslims.

We must not denigrate those who dedicated their lives to the teaching of the Name of Allah and the training and uplift of the Muslims. It will be the height of ingratitute to deny or depreciate their services. These task were performed, generally, by those who, in common parlance, are called Sufis. Do you not know what a glorious role the Sufis have played ? They have saved the Islamic society from debasement and degeneration. I can prove it. The tide of materialism would have swept the Muslim Millet away like a straw had they not performed the fundamental duty. It was owing to them that sensuality and self-indulgence could not become the order of the day with the Muslims, and when anyone succumbed to the temptations of the Devil or to his own baser instincts, he went to those godly men and repented. The Sufi saints and spiritual mentors produced the right kind of men and took from them the work for which they were most suited. Our history is defective. As I have written in the Foreword of *Tarikh-i-Dawat-o-Azimat*,[1] the fault lies not with the history of Islam, but with the writing of it. The history as it has been written revolves round the courts of kings and noble lords and no worthwhile study has been made of the endeavours of reformation and renovation, otherwise there is no vacuum in it.

Do not be misled into believing that it is only now that some persons have understood Islam. No one had done it earlier. It will show Islam in a very poor light. The continuance of the Quran will become doubtful and so will be its clarity and understandability which has been demonstrated by Divine pronouncements like *By the Scripture which maketh plain*, (XLIII : 2), and *This is clear Arabic speech*, (XVI : 103), once we profess it.

---

1. By the same author. It has been brought out into English under the title of *Saviours of Islamic Spirit*.

Moreover, how can we be sure that the book which no one could understand for twelve hundred years had now been completely understood ? I, as such, regard every book or article as harmful which gives the impression that the meaning of Islam has not fully been grasped during all these twelve hundred years or that some of the Islamic truths are yet to be unravelled. I can never accept it. The fundamental doctrines of Islam, the Quranic truths and the imperatives of Faith have always been with us, without an interruption, and whoever imagines that these have not been understood for a long time, betrays a lamentable lack of vision. I challenge anyone to prove about a reality or truth that it was forgotten at any time by the whole of the Islamic World. Ibn-i-Taimiyah has gone to the extent of claiming that there is not even a Sunnat[1] which might have been forsaken by the Muslims as a whole. If it had gone defunct in one part of the Muslim World, it was alive in another part.

Men of faith live in the world like the sun,

Setting here, rising there; rising here, setting there.

Just as the sun never really sets,—if it passes below the horizon in one part of the world, it emerges into sight in another—, the realities of Islam, also, do not become altogether extinct. If they fade away at one place, there rise up men at another place to stake their lives for the survival of those truths. Never imagine that no one has been able to understand Islam properly although it has been here with us for ever a thousand years, as if Islam is something of a riddle or an enigma. It is not like the doctrine of Trinity to explain which a complete philosophy is needed. It is nothing of the sort.

We may not meet again, and, hence, my eagerness to bring home the point to you. I do not want to blame or criticise anyone. My object simply is that the whole thing became clear to you.

---

1. Meaning a confirmed practice of the sacred Prophet.

So, have a good opinion of the pious precursors and pray for them.   It is set forth in the Quran :

And those who come (into the faith) after them and pray : Our Lord ! Forgive us and our brethren who were before us in the faith and place not in our hearts any rancour towards those who believe.   Our Lord ! Thou art Full of Pity, Merciful.

(—LIX : 10)

There is a great protection of Faith in thinking well of the pious precursors, otherwise when the tongue becomes impudent, one speaks out whatever one likes.

Brothers ! Did they not understand the Faith who were much better than us in Knowledge, Action and Repentance ? If they did not understand, how can we be sure that we have understood it ?

Another thing that helps greatly in the protection of Faith is Namaz. Do your best to offer Namaz regularly and at the correct time. As Hazrat Omar had said in a circular, "The most important in all your activities and affairs is Namaz. He who protects it, will protect everything, and he who neglects it, will not let anything remain." Thus, hold fast to Namaz ; do not neglect it wherever you are. If nothing more, offer only the Farz[1] Rakats, but it is better to offer the Sunnats[2] and Nafil[3] as well for they act as a shield for the Farz Rakats.

Lastly, beware of the Western Civilisation which is now at the peak of its glory. I have noticed here a great laxity in some matters. To put it plainly, the intermixing of the two sexes has attained alarming proportions. Try your best to avoid mixed gatherings. If it is necessary for you to attend a party or meeting where the ladies are present, maintain a distance with them. At such gatherings there should be a separate enclosure. and even a separate passage way, for women. There is a great

---

1. Meaning obligatory.
2 & 3. Meaning optional but sanctified by the practice of the holy Prophet.

protection in it. The Islamic social and cultural design is based on very wise principles and sound and healthful considerations. Free intercourse between men and women is strictly forbidden in Islam. Do not accept such influences of the American Civilisation. As far as possible, protect the Islamic culture and civilisation and try to preserve its distinctive qualities and standards.

One word more and I have done. Please do not misunderstand me. I am not advocating cultural arrogance, nor supporting a hostile or negative attitude towards anyone. Whatever I have said is in a spirit of sincerity and well-wishing. I entertain respect for everyone and am known for large-heartedness to the extent of earning a bad name. I have relations with people belonging to different schools of thought and hold them in esteem. It is out of a feeling of moral obligation that I have drawn your attention to these things.

I shall, *Insha Allah*, be praying for you and hope that you, too, will remember me in your prayers.